'A POLIC

"When constabulary
The policeman's lot

       – 'P.   *rv*. S. Gilbert

This anthology has been compiled by Superintendent G. A. Harris, M.I.P.M., M.Inst.P.S., A.M.B.I.M., Derbyshire Constabulary.

Police Dependants Trust
Patron: H.M. The Queen

Published by Police Review Publishing Co. Ltd.

ISBN 0 85164 993 9

Printed in England by Adams & Sons (Printers) Ltd., East Street, Hereford

INTRODUCTION BY
H.R.H. THE DUKE OF EDINBURGH

It is so easy to use general terms like 'The Army', or 'The Fire Service' or 'The Police' and to forget that each of these bodies is composed of people just like everyone else. Putting people in uniform does not change their human nature, it does not alter their status as parents, citizens or patients, neither do they lose the ordinary human emotions of pain and pleasure, joy and sorrow. It certainly does not deprive them of a sense of humour.

The Police, of course, have a particularly difficult time as they are bound to cause such ambivalent feelings in individuals. Whether they are seen as protectors of the virtuous and peaceful or as prosecutors of the unlawful and dishonest, depends very much on the current standing of each individual. Many join the ranks of the virtuous when the Police are engaged in preventing or detecting crime, or controlling the hooligans of the terraces, but there is liable to be a sharp switch in attitude when it comes to being caught out in a traffic offence. Either way the Police are still people.

At first sight a book of police humour seems a fairly unlikely way of raising money for charity. For a start there cannot be many people who would naturally associate the long arm of the law with anything very funny. But then a sense of humour is more than just laughing at the funny men on television, or seeing something excrutiatingly humorous in the misfortunes of others. It is also the ability to see the funny side of things even when there is a bit of tension in the air, and, perhaps most important, it is the ability to laugh at oneself, which is the best guarantee of sanity and the only insurance against self-righteous pomposity. It is quite obvious from this book that there is a funny side to a great deal of the policeman's lot.

The charity in this case is, of course, the Police Dependants' Trust, and there is nothing funny about that. We take it for granted that policemen and policewomen will take the risks which their job demands, but we cannot ignore the consequences. Death and injury are not uncommon, and that means bereaved dependants, the strain and anxiety of hospital treatment, rehabilitation and the problems of finding new employment. The price of this book may not be a major contribution to the Charity, but perhaps it will serve to remind you that 'The Police' is not just a thing, it is people doing a dangerous and difficult job, and these people also have families.

ACKNOWLEDGEMENT

If I were to recognise everyone to whom I am indebted for their help in preparing this anthology the list would run to many, many pages. Many hundreds of people from all walks of life sent me contributions – often there were duplications and variations on a theme. Naturally I could not include every item sent to me and what I have presented is my choice. What I have omitted could well provide material for a further volume.

Whether an item has been included or not I should like to extend my thanks to all those who took the trouble to send me material; I am humbled by the response I received and at the same time gratified that so many people have an interest in the Police Service and the welfare of its members.

Special thanks are due to:

Sir William Butlin, the founder of the Police Dependants' Trust, for his encouragement.

Sir David McNee, QPM, Commissioner of Police of the Metropolis, a trustee of the P.D.T., for arranging for his staff to vet the contents.

The late **D. Holdsworth,** Esq., CBE, QPM, Chief Constable, Thames Valley Police, for his welcome advice as a Police Officer and a trustee of the P.D.T.

Miss J. M. F. Coussins, secretary to the Police Dependants' Trust.

John Dunn, BBC Radio, for the coverage he gave my project.

Colin Simpson, Editor, Police Review.

No work such as this could easily be completed without practical, clerical assistance such as that which I received from Karen Leatherland and Geoff Gregory, both civilian members of the Derbyshire Constabulary.

Last but not least I offer my sincere thanks to my wife, son and daughter for their help, advice, guidance, tolerance and forebearance.

Supt. G. A. Harris

LIST OF CONTENTS

Page

TRUE STORIES

The following stories are offered as being true. Some of them I can vouch for from my own experience and from knowing the people who have related them to me. Others have the ring of truth. Some have the appearance of being true because that is the way things happen in police circles.

I have found that the same or similar stories come from different sources, reported as having taken place at different times and different places, but nevertheless they seem to me to be true; perhaps they can be classified as 'legendary'. A few are obviously fiction based on fact. Nevertheless, this section can be taken as the truth.

Cliff Michelmore, television and radio personality
This is an absolutely true story, told to me by Peter Ustinov. "Does that make it true?" I ask myself.

It was in the United States of America, when a very distinguished modern composer was driving his car down the road towards New York City. Ustinov was sitting on the front bench of the car and between them was the composer's young son. It became obvious that the composer had inspiration, because he fell very silent and the car started to accelerate – fifty, sixty, seventy miles an hour – when he was overtaken by the inevitable motor cycle cop with the hooter going WA, WA, WA.

He wound down the window and the policeman put his head inside and asked for his driving licence, which he produced, and when the policeman opened it up a 20 dollar bill fluttered out. Replacing the 20 dollar bill, the policeman then ordered the composer to get out and get around the back of the car, which he did. At which point the policeman re-opened the driving licence, withdrew the 20 dollar bill and put it into his pocket and said: "What are you trying to do? Teach the kid corruption?"

*   *   *

David Jones, Variety Club of Great Britain
On departure from a lunch at which I was present, Sir Robert Mark said to one of his subordinates: "I will be busy this

afternoon. Don't disturb me unless you have a photograph of
Carlos (terrorist) shaking hands with Lord Lucan (wanted by
police for questioning)."

*   *   *

John Thaw (Jack Regan of 'The Sweeney')

One day last summer – a Friday in the height of rush hour – we
were filming under Chiswick flyover. The scene was being shot
outside Brentford Nylons' Head Office and concerned a 'blag'
on a security truck delivering wages. Regan and Carter, acting
on information received were sitting in a car-park opposite the
factory along with other 'Squad officers'. As the security men
opened the doors of the van a car screeched round the corner,
screeched to a halt and four masked men, with shotguns, leapt
out. A little bit of dialogue ensued (remember this is *The
Sweeney,* not real) – and the villains grabbed the wages,
climbed back into the car and sped off around the corner to be
pursued by the Sweeney.

Everything went well until the villains' car 'sped around the
corner.' Then all hell was let loose! Two *real* squad cars came
from nowhere, followed by others; undercover cars appeared
like magic. The flyover was blocked off, traffic police in
landrovers came from miles away. Our poor 'villains' – actors
of course – were pursued and captured by two squad cars and
had a good deal of explaining to do, as did everyone involved.
After explanations and R/T calls it was discovered that an old
lady had spotted the 'goings-on' and rightly telephoned the
Police. Owing to a breakdown in communications it was not
relayed to the policemen involved that we were filming in that
place at that time. A high-ranking police officer's wife recently
told me that she enjoyed *The Sweeney* but the one thing she did
not like was the swearing. "Policemen don't swear," she said.

All I can say is they certainly did that day – with a vengeance!

*   *   *

Denis Norden, broadcaster, writer and raconteur

The other day I was done in Kensington for parking my car
about three centimetres over some studs marking a pedestrian
crossing. This qualifies as an amusing experience, particularly
as I was only made aware that it counts as an endorsable offence

after the policeman gave me a ticket. I said to him: "What am I supposed to do with this?" He said: "Keep it. If you manage to collect three of them, you get a bicycle."

*   *   *

John Arlott, broadcaster and author

He was a thick-headed, heavy-handed, twenty stone sergeant. In the 1930s, when jobs were hard to come by, he exerted sadistic discipline, set killer points, handed out misconduct forms like confetti; and was also the drill sergeant. He was married to a tusk-toothed woman nearly as big as himself and she ruled him as he ruled his section. They had an old Trojan car in which the pair of them sat side by side like elephants in a rickshaw. He drove selfishly and indifferently and eventually, to his horror, she decided that she would drive – and that he would teach her. Many a young constable felt some old wounds healed at sight of these tragi-comic sessions. Some even used to hide in the copse above his house to observe them in their spare time.

Her skills never burgeoned sufficiently for the manoeuvres to progress beyond their quiet side road. She was all clumsiness and errors; and eventually, one afternoon, he suggested that she should drive the car back into their ramshackle garage. She was going too fast from the start, and the large man, losing his head, let out a parade ground bellow of 'Halt'. For the only time in their life he frightened her. She stamped down the wrong foot, the car leapt over the pavement into the garage, through the back wall and ploughed ten yards through the cabbages in the garden. As he heaved himself out to inspect the damage he heard laughter – and he let out a spout of curses – but he never saw the spectators in the copse who, before the night duty mustered had spread the story to the last constable in the force.

*   *   *

Ian Kennedy Martin, television scriptwriter

A man in Lancashire, an electrician, was sitting at home one Thursday night waiting to meet some visitors to his house at eight o'clock. He had recently applied to join the Masons. He'd received a letter saying that the Masons would send someone round to interview him that night. At eight o'clock the doorbell rang and three very large men entered and one said: "I suppose you know why we are here?" And the electrician said: "Yes, I do." The first large man said: "We want to know where you keep your dirty laundry, we particularly want to see all your underpants used and unused, and all your trousers." The electrician, mystified, but remembering the historically secretive aspects of Masonry took them around on a tour of his dirty Y-fronts and trousers and dungarees.

This story is still used in the Lancashire Constabulary to instruct young detectives that they must always reveal who they are. These three men were in fact out on a particularly messy rape case in the electrician's area and had assumed from the mess made of the victim there must be blood on the trousers and underwear of the attacker. The last laugh was on the Police. Whereas the electrician was perfectly happy to stand around displaying his underwear to the three men whom he thought were Masons, as soon as it came out that they were in fact Police he went absolutely mad, threw them out of the house, and actually instituted court proceedings against them.

*   *   *

The Hon Ewen E S Montagu, CBE, QC, DL
At Somerset Assizes. A police officer was giving evidence of the arrest of a Polish miner (of whom there were many after the last war in Somerset). "I cautioned him and asked him if he had any explanation for his presence in the shop at that time of night. He made a long reply in a language which I subsequently learnt to be Polish. I told him that I was not satisfied with his explanation and took him to the police station."

*   *   *

Shaw Taylor, television personality, presenter of 'Police Five'
In a pub in a rather sleazy part of London, I was approached by a character who said "'ere Shaw, give us your autograph for my bruvver Tony will yer?" I duly obliged and he said: "Thanks a lot, I'll take it to him on Sunday, it'll cheer 'im up no end." "Oh, really" I said innocently, "isn't he well, is he in hospital?" "Hospital" said my friend incredulously, "you must be joking – 'e's in for a six month stretch, he 'ad all those stolen transistors you had on the programme!"

Michael Barratt, television personality

"My brother, who has lived in Australia for many years, has developed a dislike for uniformed policemen that is not uncommon 'down under'. Over here for a visit, he engaged in some furious arguments with me: while he fumed about 'all policemen', I insisted that the British Bobby was still a decent chap and a worthy public servant.

One day we were sitting in my car, parked on a yellow line, when a policeman approached. "Ha!" exclaimed my brother. "Now we'll see what interfering b . . . s *all* policemen are. Look he's getting out his book to charge you. They're all the same."

I wound down the window. "Good evening, officer." (I am always most polite to them).

"Good evening, Sir," he said, "I'm terribly sorry to trouble you but I wonder if I could have your autograph for my little boy?"

My brother was silenced at last!"

*   *   *

Roy Hudd, comedian

My scriptwriter, Eric Davidson, was dashing down from London to Clacton on an errand of mercy (to re-write a sketch that had 'died' in a summer show there). He was doing a fair old speed and got stopped. "Where are you off to then?" the policeman asked him. "I've got to get to Clacton to re-write some comedy material for Roy Hudd." "Get back in the car . . . I've seen the show and he needs all the help he can get."

Police escort into Clacton.

*   *   *

Rolf was a member of a class of policemen on a one-day first aid course which included artificial resuscitation and heart massage. The syllabus was a recapitulation of previous lectures, then practical demonstrations and participation followed by a group oral examination.

Early in the day the instructor went to great lengths in explaining the function and position of the heart. He finished off by saying: "Actually it is located behind the sternum."

During the oral examination he said to one of the class, "Tell me, where is your heart?" The reply in all sincerity was: "It lies behind your scrotum." The class dissolved into fits of laughter and even more so when another member of the class remarked to the embarrassed constable: "I've always said your heart was in the right place!"

*   *   *

Right Honourable Sir Harold Wilson, KG, OBE, FRS, MP

Sir Harold was in Liverpool and wished to buy a shirt. He went to a large department store which he had patronised since the days before the war when he lived in the district. Unfortunately, virtually all the shirts in the store were marked 'Made in Korea' – and similar places. Sir Harold said that he wanted a Lancashire shirt. The assistant said that they could not get them. To which Sir Harold replied that Lancashire mills were closing each week because firms were going abroad to buy.

Then, feeling that he should not take it out of the assistant, he thought he should go for the floor manager, who usually appeared for a word with him when he was shopping there. However, he could not see him. He then saw a senior-looking person in the background, went over to him and duly harangued him about the need to buy British, buy Lancashire.

The gentleman took it all quietly and Sir Harold then went away satisfied.

It was only after he left the store that he discovered that the man he addressed his complaint to was the head of Merseyside Special Branch!

*   *   *

A justices' clerk

A sergeant in the Cheshire Constabulary had occasion to stop a motorist. He asked him to produce his driving licence but the driver was unable to do so. As he was entitled to do he elected to produce it at a police station of his choice within five days. The sergeant issued him with form HO/RT/1, the official form requiring a driver so to produce . . .. The sergeant told him to sign the form so it could be compared with the signature on his driving licence.

The driver's name was Reginald Suppard and he failed to produce his driving licence within the five clear days.

The case came up at Winsford Court and the sergeant gave

his evidence after which the prosecuting superintendent handed to him the copy HO/RT/1 saying: "Is this a copy of the form you served on the defendant?" The sergeant looked at the form and then held it up saying: "It is your worships and he's signed it R Suppards.".

*   *   *

Marti Caine, comedienne
A comedian was stopped for speeding along the M1. The PC cautioned him, then recognised him and congratulated him on his talents very flatteringly. He then went on to say: ". . . well I'm sorry Freddie but I'll have to book you." To which Freddie replied: "Well OK then – but you'll have to go through my agent!"

*   *   *

Richard Baker, television personality and newscaster
People who work in television are, of course, very frequently recognised in the street, and this comes no longer as any great surprise to me after some twenty years working for the BBC. About that length of time ago, on a very dark, wet night, my car and I were involved in a small argument with a taxi in which I came off worst in that I was fined £5 for driving without due care and attention.

One Monday morning, some five years after this incident, I was driving slowly in heavy traffic along the High Street in Barnet, Hertfordshire where we then lived. A policeman on the pavement waved me down. Naturally this made me feel apprehensive though I could not think of anything I was doing wrong.

I got out of the car and the policeman approached me with the due deliberation of the law and said: "Haven't I seen you somewhere before, Sir?"

"Ah!" I thought, "he must have seen me on television." I prepared my TV face and said: "Well, I wouldn't be at all surprised, officer. You see . . ."

But before I could finish the constable collected his thoughts.

"I know," he said, "Tottenham Court – about five years ago – careless driving, that's it! Good morning Sir!"

Mike Yarwood, television personality, comedian/impersonator
It was 3 am and I was returning home from after a late night
cabaret in Yorkshire. The roads were deserted and we (my
driver and I) had been stuck at some red lights for what seemed
an eternity. We came to the conclusion that the lights must be
stuck, and proceeded very carefully to turn right. Of course the
next thing we know is that out of nowhere there appeared in
the mirror a policeman on a motorcycle, who flagged us down.
My driver got out of the car and started to talk to the officer,
who had apparently seen what we had done. The officer started
to read the riot act to him and then Ron explained that we had
come from Yorkshire where yours truly was appearing in
cabaret. Immediately the officer's attitude changed, and he
looked in the window. "I think you're great," he said,
"especially when you do Tommy Cooper." I was out of the car
in a flash, doing dear Tommy for him, and throwing in a few
others for good measure. It would seem, however that he was
incorruptable, as he took out his notebook. "Give me your
autograph for my wife," he said, "she'll never believe me."
I was only too happy to oblige. As we got back into the car he
called: "Those lights do have a tendency to stick sometimes!"

*   *   *

**Harry Secombe, singer, comedian, goon (but not necessarily in
that order)**
One amusing incident occurred when coming home late from a
show and, unable to wake the household, I tried to break into
my own house. Within minutes a police car screeched to a halt
in the drive and I felt a heavy hand on my shoulder. When the
policemen discovered who the burglar was, they broke into the
house for me and stayed for a quick nightcap.

*   *   *

**P E Brodie Esq, OBE, QPM, ex-Assistant Commissioner,
Metropolitan Police**
In 1937, having completed a course at Hendon Police College I
was serving in the rank of sergeant awaiting posting as a junior
station inspector. I was feeling rather pleased with the way
things were going for me. I was sent for by the superintendent
in charge of the Division, who was due to retire in a couple of

weeks. I entered his office and stood to attention. He looked up and said: "Brodie, you're a failure." When I recovered from the shock I said: "Sir, could you tell me in what respect I am a failure?" He said: "Sit down. When I joined 25 years ago there was crime, the primary object of an efficient police is to prevent crime. I am due to retire shortly and there is still crime so I have been a failure. When you retire there will still be crime so you also will be a failure. Now don't worry, I want to say goodbye to you and wish you luck in your career."

*   *   *

Richard Horobin, BBC television producer

Five officers were sent to a public house as the result of an emergency call reporting that a man was causing damage. When they arrived they found that it was a male mental patient who had got himself drunk and was tearing the place apart. After a long struggle they eventually placed him into a van and took him to the police station. On arrival he went berserk. Another struggle took place finishing with the man on the Enquiry Office floor with all five policemen on top of him.

A civilian telephone operator happened to pass through the office and seeing the man lying with the others on top of him she ran to the Charge Office and cried: "You'd better come sarge, they're killing a man out there." The sergeant followed her to the Enquiry Office and said to the officers: "I will have no brutality in my station, get off him." The constables protested but the sergeant insisted. They climbed off the prisoner who, in turn, got to his feet, turned around and hit the sergeant with a tremendous right hook, knocking him out. The constables fell about laughing and the prisoner saw the funny side too. He sat down, had a cup of tea and was no further trouble. The sergeant recovered but his pride was dented.

*   *   *

Sir Fred E Pritchard, MBE, LL.D

An Irish barrister practising some years ago on the Northern Circuit possessed the gift of the gab and had a merry twinkle in his eye which he used to compensate for the lack of a profound knowledge of law. Thus armed he was heard, in the course of a final speech in defence of a prisoner, to tell a jury: "My Lord will

tell you in his summing-up that it is dangerous to convict on
uncorroborated evidence of one policeman, and I say to you
how much more dangerous would it be in this case to convict
this man.on the uncorroborated evidence of TWO policemen!"

*   *   *

B R Escott Cox QC
One Question Too Many

Lincoln Assizes – civil action, one local farmer suing his
neighbour for damages for cattle trespass. In the witness box is
the plaintiff's chief witness, his farm labourer. He is being
cross-examined by counsel for the defendant.

"Mr Smith, you get very strong winds in your part of
Lincolnshire?"

"Yes sir."

"Frequently they flatten and damage standing crops?"

"Yes sir."

"In very much the way in which your employer's crops were
damaged in this case?"

"Yes sir."

The counsel paused before sitting down in triumph and then
asked the one question too many: "Then why did you say it was
my client's cattle that were responsible?"

"'cos oi never seen the wind leave cow-muck behind, sir!"

*   *   *

Three Scotsmen were on trial at the old Northants Quarter
Sessions for burglary. Their arrest in Corby by a large, plump
police officer is being closely tested by counsel for the defence
thus:

"Officer, you say you arrested three men in the middle of a
large car park?"

"Yes, sir."

"What is the surface of the car park?"

"Gravel chippings, sir."

"Did they try to run away or give any sign of hearing your
approach?"

"No, sir."

"Were you in uniform with regulation boots on?"

"Yes, sir."

"What size are your boots, officer?"

"Size eleven, sir."

"And were you wearing them that night?"

"Yes, sir."

Now the fatal question:

"How do you explain the failure of the accused to hear your approach?"

"Because, sir, I was on my bicycle at the time!"

*   *   *

Ian Wallace, singer and broadcaster
The Quality of Mercy

Many years ago, I was asked to sing at a police function in London, the proceeds were going to charity and I was appearing for nothing. At the end I was presented with an unusual and acceptable gift – a set of handcuffs (minus the key) which had been dipped in chrome. "There's supposed to be a bit of polished wood with two clips and an inscription," said the officer who made the presentation, "but it wasn't ready in time. We'll have it sent on, and then you can hang the whole thing up in your den." I thanked them all profusely, pocketed the bracelets, and the bottle of whisky they'd kindly given me as well, and went out into the night.

After six weeks had passed, I began to wonder about that mounting. It would have seemed grasping to write about it, so I tried the oblique approach. I called at our local police station and put my problem to the desk sergeant. "Mm," he murmered, "tricky. But I think I know someone in that outfit. Leave it to me."

Two weeks later, I had been singing at a late function in town. It was about 1.30 in the morning, and in those days at that hour you had the road from Lords Cricket Ground up to Swiss Cottage to yourself. Thinking of home and bed, I put a little more pressure on my right foot than the law permits and was soon waiting at the traffic lights with my nose pointing towards Fitzjohns Avenue. As if from nowhere, a dark blue limousine glided to a halt in the lane on my right, there was a sharp ting on the gong and a peak-capped figure in the front passenger seat made unmistakable gestures to the effect that he had something to say to me and that it would be a good idea if I lowered my window. I did so with a winning smile and a sinking heart. The smile was returned. "Good evening, sir, just thought you'd like to know that you'll get the mounting for your handcuffs next week. Good night."

*   *   *

A police station stood in a certain road with a small guest house next door. Over the years there had been very little trouble, then the guest house was taken over by a new owner who immmediately started to complain about the noise emanating from the police station. This went on over a period of months and the complaints got more insistent and the complainant got more abusive. Some of the noise was everyday traffic along corridors, doors closing, etc but there were also cells in the building which were occupied from time to time.

One day the owner of the guest house went into the police station, together with his wife, both even more irate than usual because of the noise which he alleged was coming from the cells adjacent to the house. The sergeant in charge said that he had done all he could to quieten the prisoner but that did not satisfy the owner. So the sergeant asked the owner if he would like to calm the prisoner down, an offer which the owner refused. The sergeant then invited the owner's wife to have a word with the prisoner in an attempt to quieten him down.

The owner was most annoyed and said, "Why should I or my wife be expected to quieten down a prisoner?" and the sergeant said, "Well, you might have better luck than we've had, it's your son!"

*   *   *

A sergeant was on mobile patrol with a constable driving through a housing estate when he saw a youth riding a motor cycle towards them on the footpath. He was carrying a girl on the pillion and had ridden for about 300 yards in this fashion when they stopped him. Having stopped the car and parked it, the sergeant got out and heard the constable speaking to the young man. He heard snippets of the conversation relating to 'L' plates and unqualified passengers. Satisfied he was in no trouble the sergeant returned to the car and was shortly joined by the constable who confirmed that the youth had no 'L' plates etc. The sergeant asked if he had reported him. The constable said: "No, I couldn't in view of his reply." He went on to tell the sergeant that when asked why he was riding on the pavement the youth had replied: "I can't ride on the road yet, I haven't passed a test".

*   *   *

It was at the local hunt point-to-point race meeting. A police constable was briefed to look after an area near one of the hurdles. There was a ladies race in progress when one lady and her horse fell at this hurdle. Horse and rider picked themselves up immediately. He ran forward and grabbed the horse's reins to prevent it running away. To his surprise the gallant lady asked him to help her remount. She presented her bent leg and he gave her a mighty 'heave-ho' and threw her right over the horse so that she landed on her feet on the other side. She said: "That was no b . . . dy help was it?" and he apologised to her. She proved to be a good sport for although they stood and stared at each other for a second or two, both burst out laughing until the tears rolled down their faces. She did not ask him to help her remount the second time as she walked away leading her horse still laughing.

It should be added that they were an ill-assorted couple, he being 6' 4" tall weighing 16 stone plus; she was 5' 2" and just 8 stone!

*   *   *

A court liaison inspector who had a wealth of experience in courts around Stafford has supplied the following examples of humour in court

Staffordshire Quarter Sessions: Counsel for the prosecution's opening address to the jury in a case of larceny: "Members of the Jury, this case concerns the theft of four and a half miles of railway line. You will see on the sketch plan that the railway line runs under a bridge *or rather it did until this man took it away.*"

Stafford Crown Court: Judge to counsel for the defence: "This is a very helpful report. It is very informative."
Counsel: "Yes, my Lord, but it is wrong."

Stafford Assizes: Judge to female prisoner with previous convictions for prostitution said: "I want you to go away and put yourself under the Probation Officer."

*   *   *

The local police were asked to keep an eye on an hotel in Torquay during the winter as the owner did not live there and all electricity, gas and water had been turned off. The owner had left a key with the police in case of fire or burglary.

Officers on patrol saw lights flickering in the windows, obtained the key and went into the house. They found that the light was from candles in bottles on the floor and tables. They searched for hippies and/or squatters, but found nothing. They took the bottles out of the house and locked up again.

The following night exactly the same thing happened.

On the third night finding the candles burning again they took them out and decided to pay a call on the owner at his bungalow.

The hotel owner said that he was very pleased that the officers had called because he was deeply disturbed about the hotel and had intended to ring the station anyway. He went on to say that nightly he had been going to the hotel and lighting candles to deter burglars or squatters or hippies, but someone kept breaking in and taking them out.

*   *   *

Some years ago, a probationer with less than twelve months service was patrolling in Pontefract which, at that time, was a rough area of the West Riding Constabulary. This probationer was only just 5' 8" tall and was small built; in fact he had just scraped through his medical examination.

Late one evening he was walking down a street and saw that there was a broken window in a cinema. He looked through, saw the light of a torch and heard someone moving about. He mustered up the deepest voice he could and shouted: "Stay where you are, the building is surrounded. He threw in his handcuffs and said: "Put those on". Sure enough the man inside complied with this instruction. "Now come out of the front doors." A few minutes passed, the doors opened and out came the man. He was 6' 4" tall and broad built, but he was manacled and went meekly with the probationer to the station, to the utter amazement and disbelief of the staff.

                    *   *   *

At the Coronation of Her Majesty Queen Elizabeth II in 1953 there was a large detachment of police drawn from all over the United Kingdom. This meant that the number of officers left for duty within forces was depleted. PC Brown was on the night relief on the day of the Coronation and it became increasingly obvious as the evening progressed that he was developing a bout of laryngitis. His throat and larynx became sore and raw and he could hardly swallow. He should have reported sick but realised how short of men the force was. Unwisely he reported for duty and was allocated to a treble beat on his cycle.

The night was hot with occasional showers which made it necessary for him to wear his cape. The heat, together with his condition, made Brown feel decidedly ill but he continued. His laryngitis was getting worse. About midnight he found the front door to the confectioners shop unlocked so he went to a nearby police telephone to ring the station. He was given the name and address of the keyholder of the premises. Off he cycled the two miles to the keyholder's address and, on his way, passed many merry-makers who had celebrated the Coronation well. He could see in many houses evidence of lively parties.

Eventually he arrived at his destination and knocked on the door. It was obvious from the noise that a party was taking place there too. At the fourth knock the door was opened. The keyholder more than a little intoxicated invited Brown into the kitchen, and offered him a drink. Brown did not drink much but with his sore throat it was like manna from heaven. "I would like a cool glass of beer or something similar." The host went away into the adjacent lounge where the festivities were taking place. He returned within a few minutes carrying a half-pint beer glass nearly full of an inviting looking brown liquid. He handed it to Brown who, with one gulp, poured the liquid on to his flaming throat. It took several seconds to happen. Brown's face went red and then blue; his eyes started to run and then he began to choke, and choke, and choke. He staggered back into a chair clutching at his throat.

The man who offered his hospitality was concerned . . . and

amazed: "You know officer, I have never seen anyone knock back a glass of whisky like that before."

It took Brown half an hour to recover sufficiently to return to his beat. However, he felt much happier when he did return and by the time he reported off-duty there was no sign of his laryngitis nor did it return!

                    *   *   *

When Prince Charles was invested as the Prince of Wales at Caernarvon in 1969 it was expected that Welsh Nationalists of extreme views would attempt some disruption on the day. Several police forces sent contingents and these had to be billetted in schools and the like in surrounding towns. One contingent was accommodated in an old school at Bangor. This contingent was two hundred strong with a chief inspector in charge and travelled in four coaches from the force area in the livery of a local firm.

Arriving at Bangor the policewomen members of the party were taken to a local boarding house. The constables and sergeants were given beds in the assembly hall and corridors of the school while the chief inspector and his four inspectors were shown to a diminutive classroom from which the desks and other equipment had not been removed. They made up their beds during the course of which the chief inspector tripped over the blackboard and strained his back. This was the night before the investiture. There were some 'domestic' troubles; the constables were dissatisfied with their accommodation, the food was hardly sufficient and one constable who 'went for a walk' became lost. The result was that the chief inspector and his inspectors eventually went to bed at 2.30 am. All were awakened at 4.00 am for breakfast prior to enbussing for Caernarvon at 5.00 am. By this time the chief inspector had found that he could lie down, sit down or stand up, but the change of state between any two postures took anything up to 20 minutes. He decided that for the rest of that long day he would remain vertical.

Breakfast finished the contingent boarded the coaches. The convoy then set out from Bangor. Some miles on the journey, just as dawn was breaking, the countryside seemed quiet and serene. The chief inspector was standing at the front of the lead coach wondering what the day had in store, what disruption would be attempted. Would his back stand up to the hours of lining the route, would there be any light relief? At that moment the driver commented that there were two hitchhikers ahead. The chief inspector saw that there were two figures vaguely discernible as a man and woman, young and obviously of the 'hippy' fraternity.

Intuitively the chief inspector asked the driver to stop. He stopped level with the couple. The chief inspector invited them aboard and they expressed their pleasure which, a moment later became a little muted when they realised that the coach was full of police officers. The man was carrying a guitar, the woman a shoulder bag which seemed surprisingly heavy! They were guided to the back of the coach and it set out on its way again.

A few minutes later a policewoman came from the rear of the coach to speak to the chief inspector. She explained that when the woman had gone to the rear of the coach space had been made for her to sit down.

As she sat down there had been a crunching, rattling sound coming from the shoulder bag. The policewoman had commented that the bag seemed heavy and had asked what were the contents. The young woman had refused to answer and had started to weep. The policewoman had felt the outside of the bag and had decided that the contents were small round objects. She had opened it and found that the contents were hundreds of marbles. The young woman had then broken down and admitted that the marbles were intended to be thrown under the hooves of the horses of the Household Cavalry when they processed to the Castle guarding the Prince. Needless to say the couple saw nothing of the procession or the ceremony and the chief inspector's strained back did not seem important.

*   *   *

At Police Headquarters the canteen facilities were very good. Constables and sergeants had their meals in the canteen. There was a Mess for officers of the rank of inspector and above.

A sergeant was promoted to the rank of inspector at Headquarters and on his first day he went to the Mess for lunch. He had soup and then the main course. When he had finished that the waitress asked him what he would like for his sweet. "I think I will have the rhubarb crumble please, Flo." Flo brought the crumble, liberally covered with custard. The new inspector tasted the sweet. It was rather strange but not uneatable; in fact he had almost finished the dish when Flo rushed in from the kitchen with an apology. The covering on the rhubarb crumble was not custard; she had taken it from the wrong sauce boat – it was salad cream!

*   *   *

Before the introduction of such things as personal radios, the constable on the beat had to rely to a great extent on the national telephone system sometimes backed up by telephones at police boxes, police pillars and, occasionally on private premises.

It was not unknown for an astute sergeant at the station to become suspicious when answering the telephone to hear the constable's voice to a 'backcloth' of clinking glasses – an experienced constable would never be caught out that way!

Local arrangements differed, of course, but in a large number of forces there would be a requirement for a constable to be at a certain telephone at a given time. He would wait there in case he was wanted and, if not, would go on his way. This would apply also at the conclusion of his tour of duty.

In one force there was a beat on which was the main fire station for the town. By arrangement between the chief constable and the fire chief, not only the man on that beat but also men from adjacent beats could use the telephone in the enquiry office at the station. Not at the same time of course. There were three adjacent beats and their times of ringing-in were staggered, except when reporting off duty.

It became the habit for the three men from the nearby beats together with the copper on whose beat it stood to arrive at the station a few minutes before ringing-in to have a cigarette and a chat.

The night relief were due to go off at 6.00 am and by 5.50 am four tired policemen were in the station awaiting the hour. It was also change-over time in the station enquiry office which was restricted in size so the four tired men had propped themselves up on the appliances in the garage.

At 5.55 am the alarm sounded and all four nearly jumped out of their size twelves. There was the sound of footsteps from above and firemen started emerging down poles. The four policemen went to the office to find where the blaze was. Within minutes four appliances were speeding down the town centre, klaxons blaring and carrying to distant parts four helmets, four capes and several pairs of gloves – all police issue!

*   *   *

Various requests and suggestions are regularly received at Headquarters. Some of them are quite bizarre. One panda car driver from a rural area submitted a suggestion through his divisional commander that all police drivers should be issued with sun-glasses, not just any type – he went on to explain exactly the type he meant.

His divisional commander, a man of no little wit, immediately realised that the glasses referred to were the type worn by a certain bald, American cop.

He submitted the suggestion thus: 'Forwarded to Headquarters for consideration. If approval is given perhaps the Chief Constable might also consider making a general issue of lollipops.'

*   *   *

The Assistant Chief Constable (Operations) put his pen through the first line of a pre-Christmas press release which read: 'This Christmas, members of the Road Traffic Division will concentrate on drinking.'

*   *   *

There cannot be many young constables who find their first appearance in the witness box to be anything but a nightmare and usually a disaster. One Sunday morning a young probationer was walking along Upperdale Road when he saw a motorcycle being driven towards him in an erratic manner. It was all over the road swerving from side to side and it was soon obvious that it was a young lad fooling about.

The constable signalled the miscreant to stop but the motor cycle sailed on past him. The constable took the number and a few days later interviewed the 16-year-old lad at his home in the presence of his father. He reported the lad for dangerous driving.

A few weeks later the case was to be heard before the Juvenile Magistrates. On the day the boy pleaded 'Not Guilty'. The prosecuting inspector directed the young constable into the witness box. It was the first time, since his training school days that he had found himself in that position – and this was for real. He picked up the Bible, read the oath and commenced his evidence: "Your worships, at 11.15 am on Sunday 23 May, I was walking Up Up Up Up . . .. The kindly magistrates' clerk looked over his spectacles and suggested: "Why don't you say 'along'?" The Constable tried again: "Your worships, at 11.15 am, on Sunday 23 May, I was walking along Upperdale Road . . ." No further trouble, but as he passed the magistrates' clerk he looked over his spectacles and stage-whispered: "A good imitation of a motor boat officer!"

*   *   *

Prisoners brought into the charge office of a police station can vary from the docile to the violent and a great deal are plain obstructive. One police station had quite a large charge office which was equipped with two large counters in the form of a 'V' with a gap at the base to allow prisoners to be taken through into the room proper; a flap being dropped as soon as they were through. They would then be searched and formally charged. After this they would pass through an iron railing also formed in a 'V' shape towards the cells at the rear. Again this 'V' had a gap at the base.

One night a particularly large Irishman was brought in by four officers for being drunk and disorderly and taking a public house apart. By the time he reached the station he had quietened down considerably. His pockets were emptied and the contents were listed; his braces, belt and shoe laces were taken from him (he was not wearing a tie) to ensure his safety while he was in the cell. He was then directed through the iron railings on the way to the cell block; it was at this point that he started to become truculent again. He took hold of the iron railings on both sides of the gap and refused to move. A struggle ensued and at one time there were three constables pushing from the rear and two pulling from the other side. They tried to release his grip from the railings, all to no avail. An impasse had been reached. The Irishman was determined to stay just where he was.

The gaoler was an ex-heavyweight boxer and looked the part. Not noted for his industry he had been seated watching the efforts of his colleagues. He slowly pulled his enormous frame from his chair and walked towards the Irishman; it looked almost certain that there would be bloodshed. But no. He walked up behind him standing with his arms outstretched holding on to the railings, and tickled him under the armpits. The Irishman, completely taken by surprise immediately released his hold and was no further trouble.

*   *   *

The local football team had won their last game and this meant that they were top of the second division of the Football League. It had been a very busy season for the local police; there had been violence in the streets before each home match, there had been violence after the match and, of course, there had been violence on the terraces normally started by a section of the home supporters, a large number of whom were readily identifiable and some of whom had been arrested on more than one occasion. A civic reception was arranged at the Town Hall and it was realised that there would be a big turn-out of the supporters. Arrangements were made for a police contingent, a large one, to be on hand.

The evening arrived and the team, in an open coach processed from the ground, through the streets to the city centre and to the Town Hall. From an early hour people had started to congregate outside the Town Hall and it was obvious that there was to be a massive turn-out, particularly when it was heard over the radio from the police car escorting the coach that a large crowd of young supporters was running along the route with the coach.

Eventually it arrived outside the Town Hall and, with difficulty, the team and their wives debussed and hurried up the steps to disappear into the reception area. It had been advertised that the team would come out on to the balcony and soon a chant started from the crowd. By this time the crowd was becoming restive. There was a good deal of pushing to get to the front and the police line, which had linked arms was pushed forward. With supreme effort, and with the aid of reinforcements, the police line managed to push back the crowd but eventually the pressure was too great and the line broke. The chief inspector in the centre of the line shouted for the line to reform. After something of a melee the line was reformed and the chief inspector pushing back found that the crowd was slowly being pushed back. He looked to his left and found that his arm was linked not with a policeman but a civilian in a donkey jacket, not only was it a civvy it was one of the crowd who was always to the forefront when there was trouble at a home match. He looked to his right and this time found that it was not only a civilian with whom he was linked but another 'supporter', this time one who had been arrested at the last game of the season and who was awaiting to appear before the magistrates. This youth looked up at the chief inspector and said: "If you're a true supporter, guv, you've got to help when you can, ain't ya!"

*   *   *

A police schools liaison officer had been lecturing to a girls' school and it was now question time.

Small girl: "Please sir, what happens to a policewoman when she gets married?"

*   *   *

Some years ago two constables on the Traffic Section of a certain force were just about to commence patrol after their breakfast at the station. As they were driving out of the yard at the rear the gaoler came out of the door of the station and signalled them to stop. The gaoler was a fan of the local football team and he asked the observer in the car if he would drop-in at the ticket office at the local ground and collect two tickets for the following Saturday's match.

The observer agreed and the gaoler handed to him a pound note. They arranged that the tickets should be handed over at the end of their tour of duty.

The first call the crew made was at the ticket office where the observer went in, collected the tickets and returned to the car. Some thirty minutes or so later they were driving along the ring-road. This road was good and wide but the subject of a 30 mph speed limit. However many motorists were tempted to exceed the limit. The driver fell-in behind a car which was moving a bit, checked the centrally positioned speedometer and saw that it was registering 50 mph. The police driver kept his car at a constant distance behind the offender for five tenths of a mile and the speed of the vehicle never fell below 50 mph.

The car was signalled to stop and the observer was out in a flash saying: "This one's mine!" He went to the offside driver's door of the offending vehicle, which had stopped just in front of the police car. The observer pulled out his pocket book from his side jacket pocket; at the same time the driver's door opened and the police driver saw two silver coins drop at the observer's feet. The observer held the door open and pointed to the coins. The police driver could see that he was telling the driver to pick the money up but the man was declining to do so. With his service and experience the police driver had come across the driver who would produce his licence with a pound note folded-up in it expecting that it would be accepted and nothing further done with regard to the offence. But to have one drop coins at your feet was something new.

The observer picked up the money and closed the car door leaving the driver sitting in his seat with the window open. The observer handed the money to the driver but he refused it, despite further heated exchanges. The observer then went through the procedure of reporting the driver for the offence he had committed. This completed the observer handed the driver a form for him to produce his driving documents later and again offered him the money; this was refused once more.

The observer, normally an even-tempered man, but one who would stand no nonsense, on this occasion lost his temper and threw the money past the driver's right ear and on to the back seat of the car, at the same time indicating that he had better be on his way.

The man drove off with much muttering, head shaking and hand gestures. The observer returned to the police car. He was livid. A discussion took place and the police driver said that he had seen everything which had taken place. "Good," he said, "two halfcrowns he dropped to the floor – fancy thinking we would fall for that – he wasn't even subtle enough to try the old one with a folded pound note; still as he didn't have a licence he couldn't very well hand it to me, and if I could only prove it I'd knock him off for bribery. Anyway I've warmed his ears, he won't try that one again in a hurry. He even said it wasn't his money and that he didn't want it."

They carried on their patrol and now and then made reference to the audacity of the offender whom they could not help regarding with disbelief as the observer had said he was quite a reasonable man when it came to reporting him for the offence.

They returned to the station at the end of their tour of duty, by which time the observer had changed with the driver. As he drove into the yard and came to rest the gaoler was waiting for them. "Did you get my tickets then?" he asked. The observer handed him the two tickets. "What about the five shillings change?" demanded the gaoler. In two seconds flat the observer had searched his pockets and then his face turned white as the awful realisation dawned on him that the two halfcrowns he had so rudely thrown into the back of the motorist's car was the change from the pound note given to him for the tickets and which he had pulled out with his pocket book. Much spluttering and explanation followed.

The sequel to this incident was that the observer wrote to the motorist and explained the simple mistake. The motorist replied with quite a nice letter and enclosed a postal order for five shillings. He was prosecuted for the offence and no mention has ever been made until this date.

                    *   *   *

It was the afternoon of Christmas Eve and the sergeant sent out one of the Road Traffic drivers in a van together with another constable to bring in two men who were reported to be drunk and disorderly in a street some two miles from the station.

As the van left the station yard there were many people about finishing their Christmas shopping, or returning home from the office Christmas party – there were many signs of the festive spirit. Girls were blowing kisses and waving mistletoe; others were dancing on the pavement. All the men seemed to be 'under the influence'.

The thought went through the mind of the constable driving that the two men who they were about to pick up would not be the only ones brought in that day.

As the van turned into the main road leading to its destination, the constables noticed a man lying on the pavement and a woman standing at an open doorway looking at him. He was lying on his side and without any movement;

he looked safe enough. The constables decided it would be better to complete their detail first and see to the man on their return journey – it would not take more than a few minutes.

On arrival at the scene they found that the two drunks who had, initially, been fighting one another were exhausted and were supporting each other. As the van stopped by them they collapsed on the pavement providing sufficient evidence for the arrest.

On the return journey to the station they found the other man lying in much the same position with the woman, still in the doorway, looking at him impatiently. The constable driving got out of the van and spoke to the man saying: "Come on then my old sunshine, you'll be safe enough with us; there's a nice warm comfortable cell for you and they'll let you out in time for your Christmas dinner."

The man looked up and said: "Why? What's up? I've done nothing wrong." The constable saw to his astonishment and embarrasment that the man was in no way under the influence of drink. He asked why he was lying on the pavement and the man replied: "I'm a plumber from the water board, this lady's pipe has burst and I've got my arm through the grate in the pavement trying to free the stop-cock!"

*   *   *

A good deal of police time is spent in escorting abnormal loads, and the problems of escorting such loads are many and varied. This was especially so in the days before motorways, one-way systems and ring-roads were so plentiful. A good police traffic patrol officer soon gets the hang of escorting such loads and very soon realises the one important requirement is to keep the load moving at an even speed and travelling as fast as conditions will allow.

A few years ago an abnormal load was to be escorted through a Midlands city. The huge load was wider than half the road but it was capable of moving at about 20 miles per hour. The road to be followed was straight and 20 miles per hour could be achieved. The secret was to be sufficiently far enough ahead of the load in order to stop any approaching traffic if necessary or to make sure that it was well on its correct side thereby ensuring, if possible, that the load's progress was uninterrupted.

The observer in the police car regularly repeated over the public address system: "Keep to the nearside please, wide load approaching." There were no problems and everything was progressing smoothly. Gradually the police car began to catch up with a middle-aged man riding a pedal cycle. The observer used the PA again and the man responded by getting as close as he could to the pavement edge and riding his cycle in the gutter. The speed of the patrol car and the load had to be regulated to the speed of the cycle. It would have been dangerous to overtake him owing to the overhang of the load. There was nothing else to do but to reduce speed and stay behind the cyclist. Gradually traffic began to build-up behind the load.

Again the observer requested: "Keep to the nearside, please, wide load following." Then, as an afterthought: "Would the man on the cycle pedal faster please?" To the surprise of both the observer and the driver of the police car the man on the cycle began to increase his speed, followed in turn by an increase in speed by the police car and the abnormal load. Further requests by the observer to "Keep to the nearside . . . that man on the cycle just a bit faster please," met with the same response until the cyclist's legs were pumping up and down like pistons and he was touching 20 miles per hour with the police car and the load lumbering after him.

The cyclist managed to maintain this speed for a couple of miles until the final request from the observer which was the straw that broke the camel's back: "Cyclist, just a little faster please." At this the cyclist rode on to the pavement and skidded to a halt just as the patrol was about to pass him. Red faced and out of breath he hurled a mouthful of good natured abuse accompanied by much shaking of his fist: "Who the . . . . do you think I am? . . . Reg Harris (a very well-known professional cyclist of the time)."

The observer replied: "Thank you sir, if you kept in training you would have left us standing!"

*   *   *

In the early 1950s the Duke of Edinburgh was resident at Clarence House.

The Metropolitan Police had a much respected chief superintendent in charge of 'A' Division, very conscientious, and it was his custom to telephone for a car late at night in order to visit his men who were posted to important posts. His nickname was 'Codseyes'.

When he 'phoned Cannon Row Garage for his police car the driver gave the tip to the switchboard operator who would, on direct lines, give messages to men on duty at Buckingham Palace, Hyde Park, Downing Street etc that the chief superintendent was about. When he visited he was delighted to find everything perfect.

One night the Duke of Edinburgh was making a personal call from the switchboard of Clarence House when he saw the incoming call register and he intercepted it. As a result of this a puzzled Duke lifted the window and called to the police out-lodge: "It means nothing to me, but it may mean something to you 'Codseyes' is on the ground!"

*　　　*　　　*

Two officials came to Police Headquarters from the Home Office to discuss a matter concerning the Criminal Investigation Department and they were shown to the office of the detective superintendent.

They immediately began their discussion and after about an hour the superintendent asked if they would like tea. They agreed and a cadet was despatched to the canteen. He returned shortly with a tray. The tea was poured while the conversation continued. They finished the tea and a second cup was offered. The superintendent then realised that though there was plenty of milk and sugar there was no hot water. The cadet was summoned. "Fetch me another tray of tea for three please, and this time bring some water!"

Within a few minutes the cadet returned with the tray. On it were three cups and saucers, the tea pot, sugar, spoons and a glass jug obviously containing cold water.

In an impatient voice the superintendent asked: "What have you brought that jug of water for?"

In a knowing voice the cadet replied: "For your whisky, sir."

*　　　*　　　*

It was constable Reader's first day on duty since returning from the Training Centre or, to be more precise, it was his first night.

He arrived at the station in plenty of time and paraded with the rest of the relief at 10.00 pm.

The constables were posted to their areas and Reader was to accompany a tutor constable on a beat on the outskirts of the sub-division. PC Bill Winters had 15 years service behind him. He was a good, solid officer, completely reliable but not over bright or, indeed, over ambitious. He was friendly disposed to everyone, particularly young constables. He was an asset. They started on patrol with Winters showing Reader everything he needed to know about the 'patch'.

Reader was also a pleasant character and eager to learn so it was a fruitful evening on all sides. Reader looked every inch a policeman; he was six feet five inches tall and very broad. Winters who was six feet was dwarfed at his side. The area was not very busy at the best of times, this night it was positively quiet. They had their refreshment period and resumed patrol at 2.30 am. Time passed quickly as they talked about their interests and families and other subjects.

At 4.00 am the first light appeared in the lowest part of the sky. They had not seen anyone or anything for an hour or more when footsteps could be heard approaching on the opposite side of the road. The footsteps were some distance away.

Winters commented: "The early starters will start coming shortly. This chap who's coming now. He works at the Post Office. Funny little chap, straggly beard always looks like an unmade bed. I bet his wife never gets up to see him off."

"She doesn't," replied Reader, "That's my dad!"

*   *   *

First aid is an essential part of a police officer's training and many continue an interest in it to the extent of joining their force team. These police teams compete locally and through regional competitions to the national police first aid competition – the Pim Trophy.

In all competitions there is a team test but each member of the team has to undertake an individual test too. All tests are realistic and very well staged.

At one test a member of the team performing his 'individual' had to deal with a man who had a ruptured varicose vein and who had had a mild heart attack. The competitor was very competent and was dealing with the emergency quite adequately. He then came to the point where he wanted to summon an ambulance.

The test was taking place in the Senior Officers' Mess of a Police Headquarters and there was a telephone on the wall with a small piece of paper sellotaped to the bottom.

The constable dialled a number and then, after a few seconds said: "Oh, I'm sorry, don't bother this is a competition." He then saw the piece of paper, dialled again and passed on his message. Shortly after a bell signalled the end of his test.

Within minutes an ambulance, blue light flashing, screeched to a halt outside the Police Headquarters looking for a customer.

The constable, on going to the telephone had, instinctively, dialled '999' not knowing that it was a direct outside line and not just an extension.

*   *   *

A lady was walking through Torquay with a particularly extrovert friend. As they crossed the central square this friend clutched her side – not in pain, but in concern because a vital piece of elastic had given way. Nothing daunted the friend walked up to a policeman on traffic duty and said: "What does a girl do in the middle of Torquay when her pants are falling down?" He didn't even blink, but said: "Come with me, madam." He took her over the road to a tobacconists, said: "Excuse me, this lady would like to go behind your counter for a minute." He saluted the lady and left. The offending garment was removed and put into a handbag to the total astonishment of the tobacconist!

*   *   *

A constable on a rural beat was well liked by most of the villagers but there was something of a feud between him and the clerk to the parish council. Nothing very serious but they were at the position where they would only speak when they had to. Neither was to blame except that the clerk was always ready to complain about the most trivial matter and then become annoyed if it was not sorted out in exactly the manner he thought proper.

One day they had a clash over some minor matter and the

clerk, because he did not get the result he wanted, complained to the inspector when he next saw him.

The inspector knew what the score was but decided to have a few cautionary words with the constable. He visited him on his beat and explained that he must be most precise and careful in his dealings with the clerk and, above all, always be polite.

The very next day the clerk rang the police house and asked to speak to the constable.

"Look here constable," he said, "this has got to stop. Someone is using the footpath at the side of my house for immoral purposes. This morning I found a contraceptive against the hedge."

"Yes sir," replied the constable, "I have taken note of your complaint. Oh, about the contraceptive, you can keep it three months and if no one claims it, it's yours!"

*   *   *

A sergeant was driving his own car on the outskirts of a northern town accompanied by a detective constable. As they drove along they come up behind a car which the detective recognised as one that was owned by a local villain whom he wanted to speak to about some crime. He mentioned this to the sergeant. When the opportunity presented itself the sergeant overtook the car and the detective signalled the driver to stop. As the sergeant slowed down the other car overtook them and drove off. This happened several times until, eventually, the sergeant managed to make the other driver pull in. The sergeant and detective, both in plain clothes went to the other car.

The sergeant asked: "Why didn't you stop?"

"Your car hasn't got 'Police' on it."

"So what?" said the detective, "London buses have 'Bovril' on but they're not full of gravy!"

*   *   *

Letter in a national newspaper:

During the recent Peace March to Trafalgar Square, I apologised to the policeman walking alongside me for possibly causing his leave to be cancelled.

"Don't worry about that," he said, "I was allowed a couple of extra hours in bed this morning. The sun is shining, and it's a treat to be with a demo when there isn't a megaphone blaring in my ear."

Liverpool Magistrates' Court – Indecent Act
After giving evidence that he had seen the defendant urinating in a public place, the officer left the witness box. He was recalled by the Chairman of the Bench, an overdressed woman of considerable local importance, who asked: "Officer, could you tell me where the nearest toilet is?"

"Yes, certainly" was the reply, "through the door to your left and it's the first on the right down the passage."

*   *   *

C H Rolph (Police Review), writer and former City of London chief inspector
A judge is a law student who marks his own examination papers.

*   *   *

During the early hours of the morning a small van raced through the town disregarding 'Slow' and 'Give way' signs. A motor patrol followed the van for two or three miles but it continued, oblivious of the police car, which was trying to overtake and stop it. Eventually the van came to a halt of its own accord. The police driver went to the man and said: "Don't you have any mirrors?" "Sorry mate," replied the van driver, "Only Express and Sun left." It was a newspaper delivery van!

*   *   *

Detective constable to suspect: "You are not telling me the truth."
Suspect: (offended) "I do not tell lies."
Detective: "You've often told me lies."
Suspect: "Ah, that's when I'm guilty, I always tell the truth when I ain't done nowt."

*   *   *

Prisoner to detective sergeant: "We carried the stuff along the canal for four miles and hid it in our garden. Them thieving lot up the road pinched it and we was getting it back when you nicked us. You ought to charge them for pinching it off us. There ain't any honest thieves nowadays."

Prostitute to magistrate on being fined £2 for soliciting: "May I have time to pay?"
Magistrate: "See what you can do in the luncheon adjournment!"

*   *   *

A man staggered into a police station in Duisburg, West Germany, threw his car keys on the desk and said: "Lock me up, I'm as drunk as a lord."

The sergeant steered him into a cell and said: "You're very conscientious."

"Nonsense," the drunk replied, "My mother-in-law has asked to visit us. Now I can't fetch her!"

*   *   *

Eltham, a suburb of London is still rather rural and boasts a harmless vagrant known as Smokey Joe. He is often to be seen pushing an old bike around carrying all his wordly goods which do not include tyres for his bicycle. On a particularly nasty November night two burly policemen investigated movements under an old sheet of corrugated iron beneath a hedge. In doing so they aroused old Smokey. He looked up at the intruders with sleep-filled eyes and said: "I pity you two blokes having to be out on a night like this!"

*   *   *

At a County Show there was a policeman on duty at the main gate. He had a radio with him and fitted into his ear was an earpiece. One of two elderly ladies going through the turnstile said to the other: "Look at the policeman's hearing-aid. You wouldn't think they would take men who were deaf, would you?"

*   *   *

A young traffic patrol officer was driving his police car on the outskirts of a large town when he saw a man sitting on a pedal cycle on the pavement and pedalling away very quickly. The driver switched on his public address system and said: "The pedal cyclist over there come off the pavement, it is an offence to ride a pedal cycle on the pavement." The pedal cyclist continued, and the driver made the announcement again as he approached. Still the man continued pedalling. It was only when the police car was about 15 yards away that the police driver realised that the man on the pavement was a scissor-grinder. The police car accelerated away.

*   *   *

A policeman on duty in Canterbury during the night found that he was being followed by a stray dog. Try as he may he could not discourage the dog from following him. His beat covered the main street and when he checked the premises of the Beaney Institute, the local museum, he found the door open. He shone his torch inside and saw that, in the foyer, was a stuffed lion and tiger. When the dog saw this he rushed in and attacked the tiger and tore it underneath. The policeman hot-footed it back to the local police station a few hundred yards away. Luckily he found a needle and thread. He hastily made his way back to the museum and, to the best of his limited ability, sewed up the tiger. Nothing was ever said – or was it?

*   *   *

The following two offerings, both true, are from an Assistant Chief Constable (Operations) who prefers to remain anonymous but whose office is in the same building as mine! As a chief superintendent I was divisional commander in a busy town south of London. One afternoon my daughter, who was at the difficult age of 18, had her boyfriend home for tea. He was very long-haired, uncouth and was lodging at an institution for youths with behavioural problems in London.

In the evening they went off for the boyfriend to catch his bus home. It was about five hundred yards to the bus stop but after an hour and a half, when she hadn't returned I got worried so I went in the car and found them both at the bus-stop; presumably some difficulty with drivers. As I was speaking to them there was a screeching of brakes and I looked up and saw a police car coming to a rapid halt on the other side of the road. A young policewoman came running across to me and said: "Are you all right sir?" I said that I was and queried why she asked. She said: "When I was coming along I saw you talking to a couple of drop-outs and you looked as if you needed some help!"

I explained to her that it was my daughter and her boyfriend. I got no further with the explanation. The poor girl tried to recover but no amount of reassurance would stop the blushes.

★   ★   ★

One summer night young Stephanie was posted to the division from Training School. She made it quite clear that she was very keen, and so she was put out as part of the night duty area car crew.

In the early hours a call came that a horse had been knocked down by a car and was badly injured.

The car arrived but on the way Stephanie let it be known that she was keen on horses and knew a great deal about them. On arrival she rushed to the horse lying in the road, and declared that the poor animal was in foal and was near to delivery.

She listened to the horse's stomach as did the policemen who had arrived with her. The men were fascinated with her knowledge and interest. So was the sergeant on his arrival. So much so that the vet was sent for to deliver the foal from the horse which was dying. After a short time the owner arrived and Stephanie blurted out what she had done and that a vet was on his way to deliver the foal and everything would be all right. The owner looked puzzled and said: "Well I don't know how that happened 'cos the bloody thing's a stallion."

Stephanie crept away and tried unsuccessfully to explain her error. Nobody knows a girl called Stephanie any more, but if you ask after 'Hoss' they will all know who you mean.

★   ★   ★

Leslie Crowther, television personality
Recently I moved from Twickenham to Bath together with my family. On our first day there the village policeman called in his Panda car. "Don't worry," he said, "it's nothing serious. I just thought I'd introduce myself. I am your village policeman.

Here's a list of useful numbers in case of emergency." He then proceeded to give me the telephone number of every policeman in Avon together with all the police stations! "Incidentally," he said, "my name is Keith Rudyard, as in Kipling." I know that from now on I shall probably call him Keith Kipling!

*   *   *

JOKES

Having researched this area at some depth it is obvious to me that, as with other subjects, there are 'standard' police jokes. You can see the same joke wrapped up in a different package time and time again. When I started on this quest I believed that I knew quite a few original tales, but my balloon was soon to be burst.

What follows is a selection of what I consider to be the best, not only of jokes of, and about, the police but also about the legal profession with which the police service must, of necessity, be for this purpose at least enjoined.

Bob Monkhouse, television and radio comedian
I heard a report that a constable and a policewoman were putting their two police patrol cars away for the night when someone inadvertently locked them in the garage overnight. Apparently it is the first time two panda drivers have mated in captivity.

*   *   *

Late one Saturday night a fellow collapsed in the street. A crowd of locals soon gathered and two constables appeared. A few enquiries and the constables obtained the man's name and address.

Borrowing a plank and a blanket they carried the man to his home. One constable knocked on the door and a head appeared at a bedroom window.
Constable: "Does Widow Thompson live here?"
Woman: "Mrs Thompson lives here but she's not a widow."
Constable: "Wait until you see what we have on this plank."

*   *   *

Ted Moult, television and radio personality
A young man and woman were parked in a lay-by. A passing panda car stopped and went over to the car. The police officer saw that the car had defective lights and he told the man that he was reporting him. He asked the usual questions: "Name,

address" etc. He then said: "What is the make of the vehicle?"
The man replied: "A Ford Courting-brake". Without thinking
the officer went on his way. Later that evening, back at his
station, he was completing the summons form when he realised
just what he had written. He realised that he must have made a
mistake. He left it until the next morning and then rang the
Ford factory at Dagenham. "Excuse me for asking, but do you
have courting-brakes?" "Not likely," came the reply, "we have
enough trouble with tea-breaks!"

*   *   *

**Eric Morecambe, television and radio personality contributed
the following:**
"I'm pleased to say that I've always been extremely popular in
London. In fact, I used to 'kill 'em' in the West End until the
police took my driving licence away."

A drunk 'phoned the police station and reported that the
entire front-end of his car had been stolen. The sergeant on
duty, though a little bemused, promised to investigate the
matter. A few minutes later the drunk rang again: "It's all
right offisher," he said, "I climbed into the back seat by
mistake!"

Here's a daft story reputed to come from a Midlands
Police Force. A woman dashed into the police station and
reported that she'd been involved in an accident with a
pedestrian. "The man I ran over admitted that it was his fault,"
she told the station sergeant, "apparently he has been run over
twice before!"

Finally, how about the young police cadet going through
training. The burly sergeant asks what he would do if a young
lady ran up to him saying that a man had embraced and kissed
her? After due consideration, the budding Dixon of Dock
green replies: "I should endeavour to re-construct the crime
with the young lady's assistance!"

*   *   *

David Hamilton, television and radio personality
Why does an Irish policeman wear three pairs of braces?
To be sure, to be sure, to be sure!

From Greville Janner, QC, MP
A foreign tourist recently asked a policeman in Whitehall:
"Which side is the Foreign Office on?"

He replied: "It's *supposed* to be on our side – but I sometimes
wonder . . .!"

*   *   *

Two tourists were standing in the Central Lobby of the House
of Commons when the Division Bell rang. "What's that?" one
of them asked the policeman at the barrier. "I don't know,
madam," he replied, "but I suppose one of them must have
escaped . . ."

*   *   *

An MP complained that the 'whipping' had been so heavy that
he could not even get out of the Commons to attend the
christening of his son. His friend replied: "You're lucky.
You couldn't be there when he was christened. I wasn't there
when mine was conceived!"

*   *   *

From Jack Moran, Past President, Association of Speakers Clubs
Police officer: "Is this car licensed, sir?"
Driver: "Yes officer, would you care for a gin and tonic!"

*   *   *

**Hugh Scanlon, past president, Amalgamated Union of
Engineering Workers**
A docker walked out of the factory gate each night with an
empty wheelbarrow covered with tarpaulin. The security
guards checked every night for 10 years, but there was never
anything in the wheelbarrow.

On the night of his retirement they asked him to explain
exactly what he was stealing, and how.

His terse reply was: "Wheelbarrows!"

*   *   *

Eric Sykes, comedian and TV personality
Policeman coming home unexpectedly and finding his wife
in bed with three men.
Policeman: "'ello, 'ello, 'ello!"
Wife: "What's the matter, aren't you talking to me?"

Her Honour Judge Jean Graham Hall
The Identification Parade
The line up is made, with the accused having carefully chosen his position with the aid and advice of his solicitor who is also present. The victim of the alleged rape is brought in, and as she walks slowly down the line, carefully looking at all the faces, the accused steps forward and, pointing, says: "that's her, that's her."

*   *   *

Alan King, FCII, manager, Police Mutual Assurance Society
One of our proposers, the wife of a police officer, intimated on her application form that she was in good health although she was 'infanticipating'.

*   *   *

On more than one occasion, in answer to questions on family history where the proposer has been asked to indicate the cause of death of a father or mother, the answer has been 'Nothing Serious'.

*   *   *

One police officer who, over a period of two years had paid over £200 premiums to a commercial insurance company (Not the PMAS) and asked for a cash surrender value. Upon being quoted a figure of £3.57 he suggested to the insurance company that surely this amount must be an error. The company replied that this was indeed an error due to a computer fault – the correct amount was £3.43.

*   *   *

A householder complained that at night walking around his garden he had received a severe blow on the head from an intruder. The station sergeant dispatched a constable who returned some 30 minutes later with an egg-shaped lump on his forehead.
   "What happened to you? Were you attacked by an intruder?"
   "No, sergeant, I stood on the same rake as the complainant!"

Motor patrol officer to erratic woman driver who is knitting at the wheel while driving: "Pull over, madam, pull over."

Lady driver: "No, no officer – a pair of socks!"

*   *   *

P B Kavanagh CBE, Deputy Commissioner, Metropolitan Police

A tourist in Ireland asked a village police sergeant how many men he had "Four, sir" said the sergeant. The visitor expressed surprise and said that he would not have thought that there was enough police work for so many men. "To tell you the truth," said the sergeant, "there isn't but if they weren't here there would be!"

*   *   *

Sir William Butlin, MBE

A policeman on his beat sees a small boy stealing sweets from a sweet shop so escorts him to the Police Station and puts him in a cell for a short time to teach him a lesson

Man in next cell asks: "What are you in for son?"

"Nicking sweets," replies the boy.

"Why don't you be clever and rob a bank?" asks the old lag.

"Can't" answers the boy, "I don't get out of school till 3.30."

*   *   *

Lord Ted Willis

From the 'Birmingham Mail': Sgt George Hampshire told a cycle thief he had arrested that he ought to be ashamed of stealing from children. The man has now been arrested for stealing cars. "I took your advice!" he told the sergeant.

*   *   *

A gallant gentleman in a Jaguar, seeing a lady on a bicycle about to ride up a steep hill offered to give her a tow. She accepted and they started off. Halfway up the hill another man in a Rolls Royce passed them gesticulating. This greatly annoyed the driver of the Jaguar who increased his speed to 'have it out' with the other driver. He was sounding his horn in an attempt to stop the other car. On the brow of the hill was a policeman sitting in his car in a lay-by. He was rather shaken by what he saw. He radioed to his control: "You're not going to believe this, sarge, a Rolls Royce has just passed me travelling at 60 miles per hour being chased by a Jaguar and there was a woman at the back pedalling like hell to overtake both of them!"

*   *   *

Richard Murdoch, comedian and radio personality

A class of 10-year-old children were asked to write an essay on the police service. These were collected in and it was discovered that one boy's essay consisted of one word 'bastards'.

The headmaster was deeply concerned by this and consulted the local divisional commander to see if something could be done to improve the image of the police service in the eyes of the schoolboy. It was decided that the police would organise a special tea party at the school. A sumptuous meal was prepared and served after which members of the force entertained the boys. Parlour games, piggy-back rides, a conjuror and many other things. A good time was had by all the boys.

The next day the boys were once again asked to write an essay on policemen.

The offending boy's essay this time consisted of two words: 'crafty bastards'.

*   *   *

The late Ted Ray, television and radio personality

Policeman: "I'm afraid I shall have to lock you up for the night."

"What's the charge?"

"No charge, sir, it's all part of the service!"

*   *   *

Man appearing in court for stealing a bar of Palmolive soap.
Magistrate: "I sentence you to a year's imprisonment."
Man: "That's a bit stiff for a tablet of Palmolive."
Magistrate: "Consider yourself lucky, it could have been Lifebuoy!"

Eddie Braben, scriptwriter

The station sergeant was having a final word with the constable before he went out on his beat.

Sergeant: "Don't forget to keep your eye open for the chap who has been nickin' ladies things from the clothes lines in Wellington Street."

Constable: "Right, sarge."

Sergeant: "Before you go . . ."

Constable: "Yes sergeant?"

Sergeant: "That mini-skirt you've got on goes rather well with your tunic."

Constable: "That's very kind of you, sergeant."

*   *   *

Terry Wogan, television and radio personality

An Englishman went to Dublin to earn his living as a 'con man'. He wasn't very successful though. The first fellow to whom he tried to sell O'Connell Bridge turned out to be the owner, and the Englishman had to give him £20 to stop him reporting the incident to the Police.

*   *   *

John Cleese, television personality

A man who was wanted by the police had been photographed in three different positions and the pictures were circulated. A few hours later a constable radioed divisional headquarters and reported: "I have arrested two of the men; the third is under observation and I hope to arrest him soon."

*   *   *

Constable reporting to HQ: "There's been a robbery and I've got one of them."

Station Sergeant: "Which one?"

Constable: "The man who was robbed."

*   *   *

In a rougher part of Liverpool a sergeant was walking along the street one night in company with the parish priest. Suddenly, a front door flew open and out ran a screaming woman. She was quickly followed by a man who grabbed hold of her, threw her to the pavement and then commenced to kick her.

The sergeant and the priest quickened their pace to assist the woman. As they approached the man looked up, saw the sergeant, ignored him, then saw the priest. He thought for a moment and then looking down at the woman said: "Now will you go to church on Sunday?"

*   *   *

The young constable was keen to get on. The divisional dinner was arranged to take place in the best local hotel and he had heard that staying at the hotel that week was the local member of parliament. Having more than his fair share of cheek, on the morning of the dinner he went to the hotel and asked to speak to the MP. He was granted audience. He explained that he was seeking early promotion and that he thought that if the MP could find the time to come over during the course of the dinner and have a few words with him it would impress the constable's superiors. Always willing to secure a vote the MP agreed. That evening the constable had managed to get himself seated next to his divisional commander. They had started the main course when the MP, passing through the dining room, came over to the table, slapped the constable on the back and said: "Hallo, Bill, how are you keeping?" The constable turned around and said: "Oh, it's you John, not now please, can't you see I'm busy?"

*   *   *

A constable was called to a house where there had been an accident. When he arrived he was surprised to see a woman sitting in a Mini in the lounge.

He said to the woman: "How did you get here, madam?"

"Oh, it was quite easy officer, I turned left at the kitchen!"

*   *   *

A constable was called to a house where a man had had a fatal accident. The body was lying in the lounge with a chest wound. The constable asked the man's wife to explain.

"Well it was like this officer," said the wife, "it being

Sunday I was cooking the Sunday joint and I said to Fred, "will you go down the garden and cut me a cauliflower. He said he would, picked up a large carving-knife, opened the kitchen door and walked down the path. Halfway down I saw him slip on a patch of mud and fall on the knife."

Constable: "That must have been a shock for you, what did you do?"

Wife: "Well, what could I do, I just had to open a tin of peas instead."

*   *   *

A constable on patrol saw a man standing on the corner of the street. He watched this man for some time. For a few minutes the man would cry and then for a few minutes laugh uncontrollably. This went on for some time – the man crying then laughing, crying then laughing. The constable went up to him and asked him to explain.

The man said: "Well it's like this officer, my mother-in-law has just driven over the cliff . . . in my new car!"

*   *   *

A motor patrol stopped the driver of a Jaguar for speeding. The constable went to the driver unbuttoning his tunic on the way and extracting his pocket book.

"Right, sir, I am reporting you for speeding, can I have your name please?"

Motorist: "Certainly, officer, Aloysious Cholmondley Monpelier Crichton."

Constable (replacing his pocket book): "Just don't let it happen again."

*   *   *

A man who was involved in litigation with a neighbour over a relatively minor matter was due to appear in the County Court. He had been told by his solicitor that he had not much chance of winning.

On the day before the hearing he went to see his solicitor and said: "You say my case isn't very strong, but I am determined to do what I can to win. I have decided to send the judge a case of champagne."

The solicitor was dismayed: "On no account must you do that. I have told you that your case is weak, but if you were to send the judge anything he would be bound to allow the case to go against you."

The case took very little time and, to the surprise of everyone, except this man, he won.

Outside the court the solicitor expressed his amazement and said: "I just can't understand how we managed to win."

"It was that champagne," explained the man.

"You mean that despite what I told you, you sent the judge champagne?"

"Of course I did, but I put the other chap's name on it!"

*   *   *

A party was being conducted around a forensic science laboratory by a doctor. They were shown into one room where there was a row of large bottles. The doctor pointed to three of them and explained that they were human brains. He went on to explain that the first bottle contained the brain of a constable and, in response to a question, replied that it was worth £50. The next bottle contained a sergeant's brain and it was worth £100. He completed his explanation by saying that the third brain was that of a superintendent and in fact was worth every bit of £200.

One of the party asked why there should be such a difference in price, and the doctor replied: "It's quite simple really – the superintendent's brain has hardly been used!"

*   *   *

A constable on a rural beat from time to time called at a certain farm. The farmer had made a good deal of money over the years and some months previously he had bought a brand new Rolls Royce. The constable had occasion to call at the farm on a diseases of animal enquiry and met the farmer outside one of his barns.

Constable: "How do you find your car then?"

Farmer: "Best one I ever had."

Constable: "What do you like most of all about it?"

Farmer: "That's difficult, everything seems just about perfect."

Constable: "Is it the upholstery?"

Farmer: "I must admit that's fine."

Constable: "The electrically operated windows?"

Farmer: "Very useful."

Constable: "The automatic gearbox?"

Farmer: "I like that as well."

Constable: "Well surely there is one feature you must appreciate better than any other."

Farmer: "Yes, I do rather like the sliding window in between the front seat and the back seats."

Constable: "Why's that?"

Farmer: "It stops the pigs breathing down my neck on the way to market!"

*   *   *

A vicar went to the village police station and reported that his bicycle had been stolen from outside the church. The constable on duty took the necessary particulars and then said: "Have you thought, sir, that it could be one of your parishioners who took it? I have a suggestion to make; next Sunday preach a sermon on the Ten Commandments and when you come to 'Thou shall not steal' look at the congregation and see if anyone's guilty conscience registers on their face." The vicar thanked the constable and said he would do just that.

A few weeks passed before the constable and the vicar next met.

Constable: "Good morning sir, have you recovered your cycle?"

Vicar (rather embarrassed): "Yes officer. I did as you said and preached a sermon on the Ten Commandments. When I got to 'Thou shalt not commit adultery' I suddenly remembered where I had left my bicycle."

*   *   *

A police car followed another car which was travelling at 50 mph through a 30 mph limit. The police officer signalled the car to stop and went to the driver who was a woman.

"I have just checked your speed at 50 mph in a 30 mph area, have you anything to say?"

"Well you see, officer, my brakes have failed and I want to get home before I have an accident."

The lady motorist had only recently passed her driving test and in any case she tended to be rather nervous under pressure. For some weeks after passing her test she had managed to avoid driving through the town centre. The day came when she simply had to go into town.

At the first set of traffic lights she stalled the car and before she could restart it the lights were red against her.

She started the car in preparation for green. The lights changed from red to red and amber and then to green. She attempted to move off but stalled once again. She was getting into a real 'flap' particularly as standing at the junction was a policeman.

She went through the procedure several times but each time, with many cars hooting behind her, she stalled. After a little while the constable sauntered round to the open driver's window and said pleasantly: "I'm sorry, madam, they are the only three colours the council have on display today, but should you have a suggested alternative I shall pass-on your preference to the Borough Surveyor."

*   *   *

A chief constable died and found himself outside the Gates of Heaven. Seated on either side of him was a clergyman. They had been there some little time when St Peter came out and explained that as there was only one vacancy at the time only the chief constable would be admitted. Both vicars protested strongly, one saying: "I have been a cleric for 50 years, surely I should be considered before a chief constable." But St Peter replied: "In his 20 years as a chief constable he has put the fear of God into more people than you two put together!"

*   *   *

Old lady to constable: "Can you see me across the road?"
Constable: "Nip across and I'll tell you!"

*   *   *

A constable was walking one night down the deserted main street of a town when around the corner came a man walking slowly and apparently spreading something about. The constable approached him and asked him what he was doing.

The man replied: "I am spreading Elephant Dust."
Constable (attempting to humour the man): "Does it keep them away then?"
Man: "Well, I can't see any around."

*   *   *

A constable was walking down the main street of the town soon after closing time when he sees three men, obviously drunk, crawling up the centre of the road on their hands and knees. As he approaches one drunk says to the others: "No matter what you do, don't give him your real name."

The constable goes up to the first drunk and says: "What's your name?" The drunk replies after looking around the shops for inspiration: "Joe Coral."

The constable puts the same question to the second drunk who replies: "Timothy White." The third drunk is far worse than his mates and when he is asked for his name he looks around in desperation and eventually replies: "Halifax Building Society."

*   *   *

A constable was posted to a new division. He had been there a few days before he met his section sergeant. When they did meet they became involved in conversation of a general nature. During the conversation the constable remarked that so far as he was concerned all the Welsh were either rugby players or prostitutes.

The sergeant said, rather tight-lipped: "I'll have you know laddie that my mother was Welsh!"

"Oh, yes, sergeant," replied the constable, "what position did she play?"

*   *   *

A patrol car was passing a public house one evening when a car pulled out of its car park. The car was driven a little too carefully so the constable in the police car decided to stop it. This he did and when he had left his car and went to the other he found that in the car was a man driver with a woman passenger and a six-year-old girl. The constable went through the formalities and asked the man to breathe into the breath-alyser, this the man did and the crystals turned green. The constable said that he was arresting the driver, but the driver protested saying that he had only partaken of one fruit juice and that the device must be faulty.

He eventually prevailed upon the police officer to try a breathalyser test upon the woman, his wife. The result was the same – the crystals turned green. The constable pointed out that the wife 'must be over the limit' too.

The driver insisted that his wife had had only one fruit juice, as he had, again saying that the 'kit' must be faulty.

"Look," he said, "let us decide this once and for all, breathalyse my young daughter."

This the constable did and once again the crystals turned green.

"That's it then, the whole lot must be faulty – on your way."

The driver started his car and drove off and as he did so he turned to his wife and said: "You know that money we spent on whisky for young Sarah was well worth it!"

*   *   *

Story without a moral: Statistics show that over 20% of all accidents are caused by drunken drivers. Therefore it would appear that sober drivers are the more dangerous!

*   *   *

Two Irishmen decide they want to join the Police Force and go to the recruiting office together. The recruiting inspector takes one into his office and tells the other to sit in the waiting room.

To the first one he says: "I want to ask you some questions. Firstly, what are hippies?" The Irishman thought for a few minutes and then answered: "Sur, I think they are the things leggies dangle from."

Inspector: "Two men are playing a game, one has drawn two lines across and crosses them with two lines down. He then puts a nought in one square and the other man puts a cross in another square. What game are they playing?"

"I'm sure I don't know sur."

"Tell me then, who killed Cock Robin?"

"Don't know, sur."

By this time the inspector was livid. He shouted: "Get out and don't come back until you've found the answer."

The Irishman left and as he went through the waiting room he turned to his mate and said: "This job's great, I've only been here five minutes, Paddy, and they have sent me out on a murder case!"

*   *   *

Some years ago in America a bus conductor who had a reputation for having a violent temper became involved in an argument with a passenger, struck him and the passenger died. After the due process of law he was sentenced to the electric chair.

The appointed day arrived and he was strapped into the chair. The electricity was switched on but nothing happened. The executioner tried twice more without success and, by the law of that state, the conductor was a free man.

Some months later a similar incident took place on a bus and the conductor was once again sentenced to death in the 'chair'.

The day of execution came and once more he was strapped in the electric chair. Once again the power was switched on without success. Twice more the executioner tried to no avail and so, once more, the prisoner was free.

As he left the chamber the executioner asked him if he knew why he could not be electrocuted and the man replied: "I guess I must be a very bad conductor."

*   *   *

Two boys went through their school days hating each other and eventually left to follow their particular careers. Some 30 years later they met on Victoria Station, but pretended not to have recognised one another. By this time one had become a chief constable and the other a bishop and both were wearing their respective uniforms.

The bishop remembering the enmity of years ago went up to the chief constable and asked: "Guard, would you tell me the time of the next train to Dover please."

The chief constable turned and replied: "I'm sorry madam, but the last train has just left."

One bright, sunny morning the vicar went for a walk through the woods. He had walked a few hundred yards when he heard a voice calling to him from the side of the footpath. Looking closely he saw a small frog. The vicar said: "Was it you who just spoke to me?"

The frog replied: "Yes vicar. You see I am not a frog but a 16-year-old prince who has been turned into a frog by my wicked uncle."

"How can I help you?" asked the vicar.

"Before I can become a prince again", said the frog, "I need to be kept very warm for many hours."

The vicar put the frog into his pocket and returned to the vicarage.

All day long he kept the frog in a warm box near to the fire. When it was time to retire the vicar took the frog from the box and took it to bed with him so that it would be warm all night.

He awoke next morning to find a beautiful flaxen-haired, 16-year-old boy next to him in bed.

"That, members of the jury, is the case for the defence!"

*　　　*　　　*

Extracts from 'The Wit of the Wig' compiled by Richard Fountain Publisher: Leslie Frewin Publishers Ltd.

Mr Justice Avory enquired whether in fact a witness had previously been convicted:

Witness: "Yes, sir, but it was due to the incapacity of my counsel rather than to any fault on my part."

Mr Justice Avory (with a smile): "It always is, and you have my sincere sympathy."

Witness: "And I deserve it, seeing as you were my counsel on that occasion."

*　　　*　　　*

In a case concerning a taxi collision, the question arose of identifying the taxi as it drove along. The witness for the plaintiff, against Lord Birkenhead, was trying to prove that he could identify the taxi and was recalling different features about it which could not possibly have been noticed by the keenest observer. He claimed to recall the colour, the make, the badge, the condition of the hood, the shape of the horn and similar features. Lord Birkenhead rose and asked sarcastically: "You did not happen to notice by any chance what fare was marked up on the taximeter?"

On one occasion, when he was judge at the Newcastle Assizes, Mr Justice Grantham left the house where he was staying, one night, to post his letters. As he was wearing a cap, he was not recognised by the police officer who was on duty outside, and the constable enquired of his lordship if the old . . . . had gone to bed yet. The judge replied that he thought not, and went on to post his letters. A short time later, he returned to the house, opened the bedroom window, and putting his head out, called: "Officer, the old . . . . is just going to bed now."

*   *   *

A young man was brought up in court on a charge of robbery. The case against had been closed and no testimony was forthcoming from the defendant. The judge turned to him impatiently: "Where are your witnesses? Haven't you any witnesses in this case?" The prisoner somewhat bewildered replied: "Witnesses? Not me. I never take along any witnesses when I commit a robbery."

*   *   *

Judge: "You are accused of stealing a chicken. Anything to say?"
Prisoner: "Just took it for a lark, sir."
Judge: "No resemblance whatever. Ten days."

*   *   *

A constable on patrol saw a car parked in a lay-by. He went up to it and looked inside. There he saw a man in the driving seat and a young girl in the passenger seat. The driver opened the window.
Constable: "What are you doing, sir?"
Man: "Reading this newspaper."
Constable: "What is the young lady doing?"
Man: "Knitting."
Constable: "What is your name?"
Man: "John Smith."
Constable: "And what is her name?"
Man: "Sally Jones."
Constable: "How old are you?"
Man: "Twenty four."
Constable: "The young lady?"
Man (looking at his watch): "In ten minutes precisely she will be sixteen!"

One of Her Majesty's Inspectors of Constabulary was inspecting a certain police force. He asked the chief constable if there were any innovations since his last inspection. The chief constable replied that he had started a vice squad, a drug squad and a serious crime squad. The inspector asked: "Have you a murder squad?", and the chief constable replied: "Who do you want murdering?"

*   *   *

There was a very heavy fall of snow in an isolated part of northern Scotland. Many villages were cut off. A joint search party of police and Red Cross personnel was formed to take assistance. They had travelled several miles when one of the party noticed a whisp of smoke coming through the snow. Obviously it was a buried house. The police took their shovels and cleared the snow from the chimney. When they had done this a Red Cross worker leant over and shouted down the chimney: "Red Cross." The faint reply came back: "Begone with you, we bought a flag last Summer!"

*   *   *

A policeman found a boy of about seven years old crying at a street corner.
Constable: "Now what's wrong with you laddie?"
Boy: "It's my birthday."
Constable: "Haven't you had any presents?"
Boy (crying even more): "Yes, I've had dozens of lovely presents."
Constable: "Well aren't you having a party then?"
Boy: "Oh, yes. My mum's made lots of cakes, jellies and trifles and all my friends are coming round and we are going to play games."
Constable: "Why are you crying then?"
Boy: "I'm lost!"

*   *   *

Chief Constable: "You joined the force when you were 19. You were selected for the Special Course at the Police College. You were a sergeant at 25, an inspector at 26, chief inspector at 28. Now on your 29th birthday I am promoting you to superintendent. Have you anything to say?"
"Thanks, dad!"

Chairman of the Bench: When the two cars came to rest how far apart were they?"

Witness: "Two yards, 1 foot, 5⅔ inches."

Chairman: "Are you sure?"

Witness: "Yes."

Chairman: "How can you be so sure?"

Witness: "I measured it with a tape."

Chairman: "Why?"

Witness: "I knew some idiot was bound to ask me!"

*   *   *

A man took his family on a day's outing to the seaside and parked his car near to the circus. On returning to his car, a Mini, he found that the top was flattened. There was a note fastened to the windscreen which read: "Sorry for the damage but my elephant mistook your yellow Mini for the box he normally sits on, please contact . . . circus."

On his return home he was stopped by a motor patrol who wanted to know why he was driving a car which was in a dangerous condition. The man explained that an elephant had sat upon it – whereupon the officer produced a breathalyser kit and said: "Blow into this!"

*   *   *

The prisoner had been truculent throughout the trial even to the extent of dismissing his counsel.

The judge was about to pass sentence but firstly asked the prisoner if he had anything to say.

". . . all," muttered the prisoner.

The judge leaned over to his clerk and said: "Did I hear the accused say something?"

Clerk: "He said '. . . all', my lord."

"That's strange," said the judge, "I could have sworn I saw his lips move!"

*   *   *

The following purports to be a question from a police promotion examination paper:

Q.   You are on duty in the High Street when there is a large explosion. This causes a large crater in the middle of the road, which is a main trunk road. The explosion blows a van on to its side and upon investigation you discover in it a man and a woman, the woman being the wife of your sergeant who is currently away on a course. Both are injured. At this point two dogs, neither of which is wearing a collar, begin to fight in the middle of the road, and they are encouraged by drinkers from a nearby public house who are quite obviously inebriated and disorderly. In the confusion a car and a coach collide and you discover that the car is being driven by your chief constable and that the bus driver has taken a shotgun from his cab with obvious intentions. A man runs from a house shouting for a midwife and a woman informs you that there is a fire in the forecourt of the large garage around the corner. You then hear someone shouting for help from the nearby canal where he has been thrown by the original explosion. Bearing in mind the provisions of The Justices of the Peace Act, the various Mental Health Acts and, particularly, section 49, Police Act, 1964, what should your course of action be?

Specimen answer: Immediately remove your helmet and mingle with the crowd.

* * *

F G Hulme, QPM, ex-General Secretary, Association of Chief Police Officers
The great Sargeant Sullivan QC defending an Irishman accused of manufacturing poteen in the wild mountains of Magilli-cuddy. The accused was put into the box and talked endlessly about anything but the matter in issue. The judge made several attempts to bring him back to the point and after his sixth and equally unsuccessful attempt he appealed to Sullivan saying: "Mr Sullivan, has your client ever heard of the legal phrase 'de minimis non curat lex'?" Sullivan paused, looked at his papers, then up at the judge and without a quiver of a smile on his face solemnly replied: "M'Lud, in the part of Ireland from which my client comes, 'tis the sole topic of conversation!"

* * *

Spike Milligan, Humourist Extrordinaire
An Irish PC in a certain London Division was censured by his station sergeant for not having charged or summonsed anyone

in 20 years. "You must try and stop crime in London, look for the law breakers, even if it's only someone urinating in the street." The Irish PC set about his task. One night he hears screams coming from inside a house, he broke in and found a man holding a knife. "What are you doing?" asked the PC. "I'm murdering my wife" he replied. The Irish PC said: "Ah, lucky for you you weren't . . . . out of the window or I would have had you!"

*   *   *

Village PC nearing retirement after 30 years' service. Looking back, he had dealt with everyone except the vicar. The vicar's habit was being late for services and he was inclined to jump the traffic lights. The following Sunday, the PC kept watch and saw the vicar riding his cycle. The lights were in the vicar's favour so the PC jumped on the pad in the side-road. The lights changed to red against the vicar who immediately braked, skidded and fell off his cycle.

PC: "I nearly had you that time vicar."
Vicar: "Yes, officer, but fortunately God was with me."
PC: "Ha, Ha – got you – riding two on a bike!"

*   *   *

Two village magistrates were reported for riding their cycles without lights. Coincidentally they were both summonsed to appear on the same day. In the retiring room they agreed that they should dispose of the summonses at the very beginning of the sitting. One magistrate went on to the bench while the other went into the box. The first magistrate read out the offence and the second pleaded 'guilty'. He was fined 50p. they then changed positions. The offence was read out and the other magistrate pleaded 'guilty'. "Fined £1." "What, £1 – I only fined you 50p for the same offence a few minutes ago." "Yes, but that's the trouble, this offence is becoming far too prevalent!"

*   *   *

A few for the children:
Where does a policeman live? Letsbe Avenue!

Why is that policeman crying mummy? Because they won't let him take his panda to bed!

What did the policeman's wife put in his sandwiches? Truncheon meat!

Policemen have numbers on their shoulders in case they get lost!

*   *   *

An Irishman in Paris teamed up with two Frenchmen to rob a bank. During the course of the robbery a security guard was shot dead and shortly afterwards the gang was arrested nearby. They were put on trial, found guilty and sentenced to death – to be executed by the guillotine. The day of the execution arrived and all three men were dressed appropriately and taken from their cells to the place of execution. The first Frenchman was led to the guillotine and asked whether he preferred to lie with his neck on the block looking upwards or looking downwards away from the blade. He chose the latter. The mechanism was released and the blade plunged towards his neck but, miraculously, when it was within an inch of his neck it stopped. The guillotine was re-set and the same thing happened once more, and on a third attempt. This was taken to be an Act of God and the man was immediately released. The second Frenchman was then led forward. He, too, chose to face away from the blade. The mechanism was activated but again the blade came to a halt an inch from his neck. The next two attempts also failed so he was released to join his colleague.

It was now the turn of the Irishman. It was his decision that he would look upwards, straight at the blade. The blade fell a first time and short of his neck. A second time the same. The executioner was about to release it a third time when the Irishman called out: "Just a minute, suh, I tink I can see where the fault is!"

*   *   *

At a police sports day there was a Tug-o-War competition between the divisional team and a team of Irishmen. The police team won when the Irish team were disqualified for pushing.

The prisoner before the court was charged with assaulting a policeman. He had grabbed the officer by the throat. In sentencing him the magistrate said: "You really must learn not to take the law into your own hands."

*   *   *

Each summer two police sergeants went to Scotland for a shooting holiday. They went to the same place each time and hired a gun-dog called 'Constable'. The first year the charge was £10. The next year, because they had been so pleased with him, they hired 'Constable' again; this time at a cost of £25.

The next time they went they once again asked for him. The owner said that the charge would be 50 pence. They asked why, after paying £10 and £25, it was so cheap. The owner replied: "Last year after you had left, another party hired the dog and one of the party called him 'Sergeant' by mistake and he hasn't got off his backside since."

*   *   *

A lady called at a police station and reported the loss of her little white poodle whose name was 'Tootles'. Gravely the station sergeant officer told her: "Yes, madam, we have a little white poodle here, but he hasn't told me his name yet."

*   *   *

A man walked into a bank with a stocking over his face, pointed two fingers at the cashier and said: "This is a cock-up." The cashier replied: "Surely you mean a stick-up?"
"No," replied the man, "I've forgotten my gun."

*   *   *

A policeman went to the police surgeon because he was worried about his weight.

The doctor said to him: "I want you to go home and tomorrow morning get up early and go for a seven mile run. I want you to run seven miles each day and come back and see me in a week's time."

The policeman replied: "I'm sorry doctor but I won't be able to."

"Why?" asked the doctor.

"Well, I'll be about fifty miles away by then!"

A beautiful young woman rushed up to a policeman and said, rather distressed: "Officer, I've just knocked down two men with my car."

"Where are they?" he asked, and she replied: "One crashed through the windscreen, and I knocked the other over a hedge into a field." "That's all right," said the policeman, smitten by the young lady's charms. "We'll be able to charge one with breaking and entering and the other with leaving the scene of an accident."

                    *   *   *

As repressed sadists are supposed to become policemen or butchers, so those with irrational fear of life become publishers. (Cyril Connelly in *Enemies of Promise*)

                    *   *   *

Our civilisation is decided . . . that determining the guilt or innocence of men is a thing too important to be trusted to trained men. . . . When it wants a library catalogued or the solar system discovered or any trifle of that kind, it uses up its specialists. When it wishes anything done which is really serious, it collates 12 of the ordinary men standing around. The same thing was done if I remember right by the founder of Christianity. (G K Chesterton 1874–1936)

                    *   *   *

Young son: "Dad, mum just backed the car into the garage and ran over my bicycle."
Dad: "Serves you right for leaving it on the front lawn."

                    *   *   *

Three men were brought into court for disorderly conduct. The judge asked one what had caused him to be arrested. "I threw peanuts into the water" the man replied. "That's not very bad" said the judge. Turning to the second man, he asked: "What did you do?" "I threw peanuts into the water too" he answered. "Well" said the judge to the third man, "I suppose you threw peanuts into the water also?" "Oh no your honour" replied the third man, "I'm Peanuts."

There are many humorous anthologies covering many subjects. Amongst the top echelon of these must be 'White tie tales', by H Mancroft and published by Bailey Brothers Ltd.

Here follows a small selection from the 'legal' section.

A man charged with stealing cars was told by the magistrates that he could be tried by his peers or be dealt with by the magistrates.

"What do you mean by peers?" asked the man and was told: "Peers are your equals, men of your own class and own kind." "You try the case," promptly replied the accused, "I don't think I want to be tried by a bunch of car thieves."

*   *   *

The late Mr Ernest Marples

In the House of Commons I have a certain view of solicitors. I remember talking to some people from South Africa in Westminster Abbey as they were looking at some monuments of great men. I said to them: "There lies a lawyer and an honest man." One member of the party replied: "Since how long has it been the custom in this land to bury two people in one grave?"

*   *   *

Sir Noel Bowater, sometime Lord Mayor of London

A man about to be sentenced at the Old Bailey for a serious offence who was asked by the clerk if he had anything to say before judgement was passed, replied: "God strike me dead if I am guilty." The judge sat in silence for a moment or two and then addressing the prisoner, said: "Providence not having seen fit to intervene in your case it now becomes my duty to do my humble best to see that justice is done."

*   *   *

Sir Godfrey Russell Vick, QC

A fellow was driving along a country lane in a pony and trap when there was a collision with a motorist. The pony and trap overturned into a ditch. The fellow claimed damages and there was a sequel in court against the motorist. Cross examination of the fellow went like this:

Counsel for the motorist: "Is it not right that after the accident you told the motorist that you were all right?"

Pony driver: "That is difficult to answer."

Counsel: "Surely you can answer yes or no to that simple question?"

The judge wisely intervened saying: "Tell the court what happened."

Pony driver: "Well, the motorist hit me and drove on. He came back and found the pony in the ditch. He said: "Poor beast, he has two broken legs," and pulled out a gun and shot it dead. Then he turned to me and asked if I was all right. I said I was!"

*   *   *

A jury in a criminal court retired to consider their verdict. They returned in an hour and asked the judge whether the prisoner had chosen his counsel himself or whether he had been appointed by the court. The judge, puzzled, said the accused had chosen his counsel himself. The foreman then turned round and looked at the rest of the jury all of whom nodded their heads. "We find the prisoner insane," he told the judge.

CARTOONS

I suppose it is fair comment to say that of all subjects which come to the cartoonist's pen, amongst the most frequent must be the policeman, usually with enormous paunch, glowing nose and size fourteen boots. Yet, on the whole, over recent years at least, cartoonists have been relatively kind.

In this section famous cartoonists are joined by people who draw cartoons as a hobby; all are excellent.

Also included are examples of that British seaside tradition which ranks second only to seaside rock – the seaside postcard.

(Nothing is sacred! No-one is safe from the cartoonist. A short time before I commenced my research I had a slight accident in my car. Turning from a major road into a minor road I happened to come into contact with the front wheel of a bicycle. It was being held by a constable waiting, quite correctly, to emerge from the minor road. The only damage was to the front wheel – it was a police-owned cycle. It was not very long before a cartoon appeared on my desk from the force cartoonist – every force has one! The contribution is the first in the following collection.)

" FOLLOW THAT CAR "

"You say it all stems from your unhappy childhood. Your mummy wouldn't let you have a teddy ... [and after you decided to beat a policeman in the face]"

"Now, men! Your new uniforms for duty at the next Notting Hill festival are designed to ensure you don't look 'provocative' . . ."

"Relax, they're mine."

WHO WAS DRIVING THE VEHICLE?
'NONE OF US CONSTABLE — WE WERE ALL IN THE BACK!'

"There we are, boys—'PORNOKIT!'"

'How much further to your fancy dress party?
We've already had 25 heart attacks reported.'

THE
JOHN DUNN SHOW

I have said elsewhere that my gratitude is due to many, many people for their contributions and it would not be right of me to single out, except where necessary, specific contributors. Nevertheless, it would not be right to ignore the response I had through the efforts of John Dunn on his Radio Two programme. The next chapter includes a cross-section of items submitted to John and forwarded to me.

*   *   *

The following events are reputed to have taken place in Edinburgh a few years ago. A young lady learner driver was having difficulty moving away from the traffic lights when they changed to green. After several attempts, always ending in the engine stalling, and after several changes of lights, the following tailback of vehicles gradually peeled off into other lanes and eventually cleared the junction; all except for one, a police car, which had been immediately behind the learner. It was obvious that both the driver and the instructor were becoming frustrated and, in an effort to calm the situation, the driver of the patrol car called instructions over the public address system, much to the amazement of the learner and the instructor and also to the many passers-by.

Acting upon the instructions the lady manoeuvered the gear lever, the clutch pedal and the accelerator in complete synchronisation, except that she selected reverse gear. Sudden acceleration and the car reversed into the patrol car with a resounding crash of metal and glass. The air was filled with abuse from the police driver **who had forgotten to switch off the PA!**

*   *   *

The following appeared in 'Berrow's Journal', a Worcester newspaper which claims itself to be the world's oldest newspaper:

"Droitwich councillor Jean Brackston came close to being

the first victim of her own 'anti-parking' campaign when she popped down to the launderette and parked in Rickett's Lane.

Mrs Brackston insisted at a Wychavon council meeting that parking along Rickett's Lane caused serious congestion, and as a result Hereford and Worcester County Council is being urged to put a 'No Waiting' order there. And when Mrs Brackston came out of the launderette a police car was waiting.

'Do you know we could book you for five different traffic offences?' asked a stern faced policeman, who reeled off a list including parking on the wrong side of the road and within 15 feet of a road junction. 'I'm very sorry,' said Mrs Brackston. 'But it's so wet I tried to park close to the launderette.'

The policeman said that on this occasion she would be let off with a warning, but they were having to keep a special eye on the lane because of parking complaints from a local councillor! 'She's a real nuisance you know. She's been making a tremendous fuss about this lane on the council,' he added.

The policeman got back into his car with his colleague who looked up and said: 'Goodnight Councillor Brackston'.''

*   *   *

One evening a constable called at a house to notify a dog owner that her pet had been found and was ready for collection from the police station. It was a summer evening and the owner lived in a bungalow on a housing estate. The constable knocked on the door but could get no reply, although he could hear movement inside, so he continued knocking. He had no success so he bent down to the letterbox and opened it with the intention of shouting through. As he opened it he was more than a little surprised to see a large lady, at least 18 stone, stark naked, crawling on her hands and knees towards the door. The lady had obviously been in the process of bathing as clouds of steam surrounded her progress. The constable endeavoured to deliver the message regarding the dog only to discover that she was deaf. He knelt down at the door and shouted into her ear and eventually she understood. However, by the time he had completed his mission, a crowd had gathered and was greatly amused at the sight of a policeman shouting through a letterbox, with clouds of steam issuing out into the street!

The following contribution was supplied by John Jordan of the Metropolitan Police whose experience it is. It has been previously published in a Met magazine edited by Peter Simmons.

"I had not been in the job all that long. Nevertheless, I had reached the stage of not looking for trouble – or anything else, come to think of it.

The suburbs of Paddington, if you can call them that, had the unusual knack of getting one involved when one least expected it or wanted it. Even the journey on foot in uniform back to the section house could lead directly to court the following morning. So when the next day is weekly leave and everything is planned for a good day's relaxation, the idea is not to look too closely, become a little deaf, and pretend to be heading somewhere urgently.

It was half-past eight in the evening. Autumn had shaken its leaves over summer and put out the sunlight. The street lights were augmented by their reflections in the damp and grease on the roadway. The Mini drew up alongside me, and the passenger's window was opened. I naturally decided that it was not a policeman the occupants were looking for so I quickened my step and carried on. A Mini being driven too far in first gear is not a pleasant sound. It is worse when it is catching up a reluctant copper. It was me they wanted. I had felt it when they were yards away. My weekly leave on the morrow had told me so. What would it be? A drunk by the side of the bridge, a non-swimmer in the canal who had been there for hours? I did so much want to get away spot on ten that night. Perhaps some female was about to give birth? Who cares? It was bound to be something which would get me involved past ten o'clock.

I put on my best 'I don't like Mini-drivers face' and glowered at the passenger in the Mini – now right beside me. Perhaps he would be a member of the anti-police club and go away. I was wrong. In the first place, she was a female – and second, she did not go away. I cannot say I objected too strongly, she was wearing a lovely low-cut dress and her skirt was hitched-up. I am a sucker for a pretty face – even to this day. I smiled and became my old James Bond self again. 'Can I help you?' I said hypocritically.

She obviously knew I was the wolf type and breathed deeply.

'You handsome pig', I thought, 'she's going to invite you to a party or something.'

'Do you have braces?' Her question set my mind galloping. Fast, pretty bitch.

'Yes, of course,' I replied trying to be suave.

'Where are they?' she asked coquettishly.

'Holding up my trousers,' said I.

'Could I borrow them, please?' I knew then that she fancied me. She must have heard of me from one of my conquests. The way she looked at me – she could have the trousers as well. I was working out some really clever, pertinent comment when the driver leaned across. It never crossed my mind that she would be escorted.

'I hope this does not seem silly officer, but it is a genuine request.' He was taller and better looking than me. I disliked him intensely. The dish with him had hooked me, fool that I am. I had to be polite now.

'It's an odd request, sir,' I said, 'besides I need them to hold up my trousers.' I began to suspect some ulterior motive. There was a school for medical students nearby.

'Yes, it is unusual,' he said patronisingly, 'you see we are going to a dinner and I must have some braces to hold up my trousers.' He should worry. I had to walk the streets of London, and I did not want to set a precedent. There would be questions in the House. He was in evening garb and suited it.

'I'm afraid it's out of the question, sir, I don't finish until ten and you can hardly expect me to walk round in uniform with my hands in my pockets.' I have always considered myself quick with a funny line. He forced himself and smiled. 'You could use this.' He handed across a tatty, old, grey cloth belt which he had taken quickly from his waist. I should have been much firmer. Here I was with the transaction practically completed against my better judgement. My hand brushed against the delicious girl as I put it through the open window and collected the belt. She smiled into my eyes. I thought that it was a bit unlucky for the chap having to go to a dinner without something to keep him smart and his trousers secure at the same time. How he had got into such a fix was beyond my thoughts just then. I started thinking about letting him have them. I know we London policemen are wonderful – but this was going a bit far.

'I'm sorry. I cannot possibly undress in the street here.' I

pushed the belt back through the window. His girl leaned back
out of the way of my hand this time.

'How about the police station?' he said. 'It's just over the
bridge.' He was right. It was. She smiled. I lost.

'OK. Go to the door next to the main entrance.' This led to the
canteen and stripping would be less conspicuous there. We did
the swop and he zoomed off. I never saw him again. For the last
hour and ten minutes of my duty I did not wander too far from the
station. If I felt my trousers going then sanctuary had to be close
at hand. I had my day off. Nothing spoiled it. The day after a
parcel arrived through the post. In it was a pair of red braces
and twenty cigarettes. I wonder if he had a good night out.
That tall, good looking, smart (thanks to me), lucky devil!"

*   *   *

A young and recently appointed police constable's beat was in a
residential district of South London.

One evening a dear old lady approached him in the street to
say that she had lost her cat which was brown and white and
should he find it would he please take it to No 25 and put it
through the window over her front door which she would leave
open for him.

The constable then returned to his station to have supper
and, rather unwisely as it transpired, said to his colleagues that
should any of them find the cat would they put it through the
lady's window.

Next evening when he was again patrolling the street the little
old lady was waiting for him and said very sweetly: "Thank you
officer for all the trouble you have taken. At least twelve cats
have been put through my window – but not one of them is
mine!"

*   *   *

A police sergeant was hailed as being a hero by the community
for saving a young lad from drowning in the local river. For his
bravery he was presented with a gold watch. It was revealed
later, however, that the lad had been chased into the river in
the first place by the sergeant who was trying to arrest him!

An errand boy, working for a butcher in London. His job was to deliver meat to various customers on a trades bicycle. One day he was told to collect a dead pig from a neighbouring butcher's shop.

The dead pig was placed into the basket of the trades bicycle, with its head and two front trotters resting over the front of the basket. He then made his way back to his shop, pushing hard on the pedals as the pig was heavier than he.

As he approached the main road junction a policeman on point duty held up his big hand, looked down at him, and the pig in the basket, and said: "Now then lad. If you two want to ride on a bike get yourselves a tandem!"

*   *   *

A lorry was passing Arundel Police Station carrying mouldings and started up a slight incline when the load slipped off the lorry. A young constable came out of the station and said: "Bad luck, mate, I'll help you re-load it." After a while the station sergeant knocked on the window and beckoned to the policeman to return into the station. A few moments later he re-emerged and said to the driver: "Sorry mate, I've got to book you for having an insecure load."

*   *   *

The following is an extract from a book 'Cycling is my life' written by the famous cyclist Tommy Simpson and published by Stanley Paul of London, in 1966.

After spending his first year abroad as a professional, Tommy was returning home to get married and was travelling in an Aston Martin DB2, a recent acquisition of which he was very proud.

"I drove back, enjoying my car, and took the road from Dover without a care in the world. As I was approaching Newark I noticed there was a big traffic hold-up going into the town. I knew Newark from my early cycling days and realised that the level-crossing gates were closed. I swung the wheel over and drove along the right hand side of the road, past the big queue of traffic.

I reasoned that by the time I reached the gates they would be opening and I would be able to slip in somewhere and knew that no traffic would be coming the other way. I should have known that my luck was not good, and as I approached the gates they were still firmly shut. I slowed down, and as I got near to the front of the line I saw, to my horror, that a police car was second in line. I pulled the left-hand drive Aston Martin to a stop alongside the police car and, pretending not to notice, stared straight ahead feeling my face going slightly red at the same time!

The police driver wound down his window and pushed his head out towards me. "What do you think you're doing?" he asked crossly, "don't you realise you are on the wrong side of the road?" Using my hands expressively I turned to him and replied: "Non!" He took a quick look at my left-hand drive and said: "Another bloody Froggie!" and waved me on as the gates opened. Phew! I was pleased he had not asked for my passport!"

*   *   *

He was a small man and lived in a little semi-detached house. He had a garden and was determined he was going to have the best and biggest produce from the garden. With this in mind he set out to collect some horse manure from the nearby race-course so, together with his son, he set off early one dark and foggy morning on their cycles armed with a shovel and a couple of sacks.

Having filled these sacks they put them on the crossboys and started on their way back. Passing through a partly-built housing site – from which there had been many thefts – they met the local bobby.

"What have you in there?" he asked.

No reply.

"I intend to look in that sack, sir, so don't be difficult!"

The man untied his sack and the constable plunged his hand straight in to the bottom – no doubt expecting to find stolen sand or cement. He withdrew his hand and his jaw dropped!

A HUMOROUS
MISCELLANY

I received many contributions which do not fit easily under any special heading, but, nevertheless, are every bit as important to a book covering the whole subject. Here follows a selection.

Ronnie Barker, comedian, offers the following monologue, taken from the television show 'The Two Ronnies'

> "If it wasn't for us coppers
> Where would the country be?
> The p'liceman's job is to protect
> The likes of you and me
> For crooks are people, just like us,
> It's clear what I must do
> I must go out and stop myself
> From robbing me and you.
>
> If the copper stopped patrolling
>   all along his usual beat
> There'd be big piles of old ladies
>   on the same side of the street
> We'd all drive dreadfully without
>   the p'lice to show us how
> And traffic jams would **almost** be
> As bad as they are now.
>
> If it wasn't for us coppers, drunken
>   driving would be rife
> And the poor old drunk pedestrian would,
>   be running for his life.
> So if some cold night one stops you
> In your Bentleys or your Jags
> Give the chap a bit of pleasure,
> And breathe into his bags.

If it wasn't for us coppers, there'd be
  no sports display
With all those trained Alsations, to
  brighten up our days;
There'd be no social functions; there'd be
  no fun at all,
For if there's no police you couldn't hold
  a policeman's ball.

So when a copper passes you, with firm
  and measured tread
With his noble pointed helmet on his
  noble pointed head,
Whether lunching with the Lord Mayor,
  or sitting on the loo,
Just give a thought to us chaps, and
  salute the boys in blue.

      ★   ★   ★

**The following Odd ode is from 'Odd Odes and Oddities' and is
included in this anthology by kind permission of Cyril Fletcher
and the Publishers, Galaxy**

This is the tale of Sally Small,
Proud owner of a market stall.
She sold plates of luscious whelks,
Prawns and winkles in their shelks (sorry rhyme)
And youngsters too came in their masses
For her crustacean delicacies.
Then came a time, and here's the rub
When the landlord of her local pub
Put on a show of which the star
Danced topless in the Public Bar.
And all Sal's customers forsook'er
To see the topless one's basooker.
Now Sally faced a hideous fate
She couldn't sell a single plate.
"How can I sell a single prawn
Now all my customers are gorn
Down to that disco bar

To soak up beer and oo la la?"
For the next episode we thank
The manager of Sally's bank
Tearfully she begged a little loan,
"Until that crowd of over grown
Schoolboys get tired of topless trollops
And come back to me and scoff my scollops."
Sternly the manager said "No!
You'll have to stimulate cash flow;
Your assets up to now concealed
Must now be totally revealed.
Madam compete", he added flat,
"You fight for custom, tit for tat.
"Ponder", he added, "Then I trust,
See the solution, bust or bust.
That's my advice, how does it strike you?"
"Oo you are awful but I like you."
Said Sal and then confessed,
"Even me crabs was served up dressed.
I can't close the stall and give them best,
I'll keep with changing trends abreast."
"Out of the old and into the blue,"
Sang Sally seeing trade renew.
Each customer to get a glimpse
From Sally bought a plate of shrimps.
A policeman came and parked his bike
Saying, "I've not never seen the like.
We must point out Madam, pursuant to
Street Trading Acts 19 HO 2,
A ten pound fine must be recovered
On all dishes found uncovered."
He looked at her o'er crabs and fish,
And thought, "You are a luscious dish.
Too long, my darling, we have tarried."
Two weeks later they were married.

                    *   *   *

**I am delighted to be able to include the following 'ode'. It was
sent to me by Edward J Darby, from North Kensington. In his
letter to me he says "As an Old Contemptable of 85 I find much**

pleasure in the writing of humorous odes as a recreation in the autumn of one's life."

'Tarred'

This is the tale of Constable Drew
The finest man that ever wore blue.
One day they took him from his beat,
To direct the Traffic in High Street,
And he was feeling all forlorn
For on each foot he had a corn.
It was a hot and scorching day,
Standing in that main highway
And as he stood upon the ground,
The tar was melting all round.
Soon he felt his feet were baking
With the heat the tar was making.
He tried his best to ease the pain,
By letting each foot take the strain.
He said: "I'll have to change this spot
It's getting really quite too hot.
He tried to move but quickly found
That he was rooted to the ground.
Then he said: "Cor, luv a duck,
I do believe my feet are stuck."
The roadway oozed with melted tar
Churned up by each passing car.
And as they passed at rapid pace
They squirted hot tar in his face.
The sergeant coming on the scene
Said: "Are you acting for the screen
Your face looks a perfect sight
Just like the minstrels Black and White."
Then summing-up the situation
Said: "I'll have to phone the station
To free you from your sorry plight
Or else you'll be here half the night.
Help arrived but soon it proved
That not an inch could he be moved.
Another effort must be made
And so they 'phoned the Fire Brigade.
Crowds had gathered from all quarters
Television and reporters,

For they all had come to see
The rescue of that poor PC.
To swell the crowd there came road menders,
Ice Cream carts and Peanut Vendors,
And just outside the old Town Hall
Someone had opened a coffee stall
Where to everyone's surprise
Was busy selling hot meat pies.
He even sent a cup of tea
To quench the thirst of that poor PC.
The firemen worked with might and main
With slings and ropes and mobile crane.
Whilst cars were belching fumes and smoke
Causing half of them to choke
And as the fumes got gradually worse
They fetched a doctor and a nurse.
Then amidst their scarlet faces
A boy bent down and cut the laces.
So at last they did succeed
In getting that poor policeman freed.
The crowd then gave a loud 'Hurrah'
And Constable Drew said: "Thank you . . . Ta!"

*   *   *

The late Sir Derrick Capper, QPM, Chief Constable of
Birmingham City and, later, West Midlands Police, was noted as
a raconteur and after-dinner speaker. He passed to me the
following quotes about the Law & Lawyers.

If you laid all our laws end to end, there would be no end.
                                    Arthur Baer (USA)
It is impossible to tell where the law stops and justice begins.
                                    Arthur Baer
Lawyers are the only persons in whom ignorance of the law is
not punished.

                                    Jeremy Bentham
A lawyer is a learned gentleman who rescues your estate from
your enemies and keeps it himself.

                                    Henry Brougham

Law and equity are two things which God hath joined but which man has put asunder.

Charles Caleb Colston

Lawyers are the only civil delinquents whose judges must, of necessity, be chosen from themselves.

Charles Caleb Colston

I sometimes wish that people would put a little more emphasis upon the observance of the law than they do upon its enforcement.

Calvin Coolidge

If there were no bad people there would be no good lawyers.

Charles Dickens

The law, in its majestic equality, forbids the rich as well as the poor to sleep under bridges, to bed in the streets and to steal bread.

Anatole France

God works wonders now and then; behold, a lawyer, an honest man.

Benjamin Franklin

A successful lawsuit is the one worn by a policeman.

Robert Frost

If the laws could speak for themselves, they would complain of the lawyers in the first place.

Marquis of Halifax (1633/95)

A man may as well open an oyster without a knife as a lawyer's mouth without a fee.

Barten Holyday (1593)

Lawyers earn a living by the sweat of their browbeating.

J G Huneker

I was never ruined but twice; once when I lost a lawsuit, and once when I won one.

Voltaire

*   *   *

Rt. Hon. Lord 'Manny' Shinwell, PC (not Police Constable), CH, DCL offered the following. (I believe that he had his tongue firmly in his cheek).

. . . "an incident concerning the police of a humorous character I am unable to recall. As for other incidents, they are associated with political events and cannot be condensed in a form easily understood by those outside the political arena. I must therefore ask to be excused, but must express my admiration about your project. I only wish that viewing world affairs as I have to do, and in particular the effect on our country it was possible to discover anything of amusement. If you can, your service to society would deserve at least the George Cross."

(The sting, or pun, is in the tail!)

* * *

I am grateful to Alan King, FCII, Manager and Secretary of the Police Mutual Assurance Society and his staff for the following collection of howlers taken from accident insurance claims submitted to many companies.

1. The accident was due to the other fellow narrowly missing me.
2. Cow wandered into lorry. I was afterwards informed that the cow was halfwitted.
3. Lorry driver bolted and worked for corporation.
4. My car was pinched and I set up a human cry but it has not come back.
5. A lamp-post bumped my car bending it in two places.
6. She suddenly saw me and lost her head.
7. A lorry backed through the windscreen into my officer's face.
8. I remember nothing after the 'Haycock' until I came to and saw PC Brown.
9. I told the other idiot what he was and went on.
10. I knocked over the man; he admitted it was his fault as he had been knocked over before.
11. I bumped a lamp-post which was hiding behind a human being.
12. Dog on the road applied brakes, causing a skid.
13. I collided with a stationary tramcar which was coming in the opposite direction.
14. I misjudged a lady crossing the road.
15. I left my car unattended for a few minutes and whether by accident or design it ran away.
16. I collided with a stationary tree.
17. I was scraping my rearside on a bank when the accident happened.

18. I heard a horn blow and was struck in the back – evidently a lady was trying to pass me.

19. Coming back, I took the wrong turning and drove into a tree that was not there.

20. A working gentleman offered to be a neutral witness in my favour.

21. I thought the side window was down, but it was up, as I found when I pushed my head through it.

22. There was no damage to the vehicle, as the gate-post will testify.

23. I was keeping two yards from each lamp-post, which were in a straight line, unfortunately there was a bend in the road bringing a right-hand lamp-post in line with the others and of course I landed in the river.

24. To avoid a collision I ran into the other lorry.

25. My vehicle plunged down the bank, landing in the railway, I trust this meets with your approval.

26. I blew my horn, but it had been stolen, and would not work.

27. A bull was standing near and a bee must have tickled him, as he gored my car.

28. Lorry had to turn sharply to avoid an invisible car.

29. If the other driver had stopped a few yards behind himself nothing would have happened.

30. Accident was due to the road bending.

31. The witness gave his occupation as a gentleman.

32. I consider neither vehicle was to blame, but, if either vehicle was to blame it was the other one.

33. On entering Scotland I blew my horn at the left hand corner.

34. There were plenty of lookers-on but not a decent witness.

35. Three women were all talking to each other, and when two stepped back and one stepped forward I had to have an accident.

36. Whilst waiting at traffic lights I was rammed by the stationary car behind me.

37. I was having a dispute with my wife, she pulled my hair causing me to turn into a lamp standard.

38. I am not sure who was responsible for the accident but there are plenty of suspects.

39. The car owner turned and cut my head off.

40. The Third Party skidded across the road and ripping up the concrete and sticking the circle and stopping when it was jammed between telegraph pole and hedge.

41. I went to see a friend when the accident occurred about a little business.

42. I reduced the waling space and just skinned him.

43. I was crossing from Edgware Road to Park Lane in the direction of Margate.

44. I collided with a dog avoiding a lamp-post.

45. I slept in the tramlines and skidded on Wednesday.

46. The other man turned into a coal sack.

47. I did not take the names of the witnesses as in their ignorance they said I was to blame.

48. I am not known to any of the parties, my evidence is therefore immaterial.

49. If my offer of settlement is not satisfactory you must take it out of my wife, I will pay more when I am doing more time.

50. I sounded my horn, the pedestrian ran for the pavement, but I got him.

51. They drove past while I was turning with my red light out. They were going fast and did not see it and hit their back part very slightly near my engine.

52. One wheel went into the ditch, my foot jumped from the brake to the accelerator pedal, leapt across to the other side, and jammed into the trunk of a tree.

53. I left my Austin Seven outside, and when I came out later, to my amazement there was an Austin Twelve.

54. The other man altered his mind so I had to run into him.

55. I can give no details of the accident as I was somewhat concussed at the time.

56. Wilful damage was done to the upholstery by rats.

57. A pedestrian hit me and went under my car.

58. I ran into a shop window and sustained injuries to my wife.

59. Coming home, I drove into the wrong house and collided with a tree I haven't got.

60. The other car collided with mine without giving any warning of its intention.

61. I didn't see the other car, but I noticed it was travelling too fast.

62. The car occupants were stalking deer on the hillside.

63. The water in my radiator accidentally froze at twelve midnight.
64. I unfortunately ran over a pedestrian and the old gentleman was taken to hospital much regretting the circumstances.
65. A pedestrian crossing the road was caught by a car – owzat!
66. Female woman hit by car celebrating New Year in roadway.
67. Driver leaned forward to swat a fly on the windscreen and hit the car in front.

*   *   *

Several police forces publish their own newspaper or magazine. Among the best, if not the best, must be 'Guardian' published by the Strathclyde Police. It is a particularly well presented magazine, at least the equal of many nationally published professional magazines. Here follows a selection of contributions from its columns.

I HATE CIVILIANS

I hate civilians! I married one! I wish I had married a police-woman. At least my wife would be working. She hasn't worked since the day we got married. Civilians don't appeal to me at all. My mother is a civilian. She keeps asking me when I am going to get a decent job and stop persecuting poor motorists! My dentist is a civilian. He drills big holes in my teeth and keeps asking me why the police persecute motorists and won't let them park on yellow lines. It's not that he hurts me, it's just that I am never sure if he intends to! The minister in our church is a civilian although he tries to hide it by wearing a kind of uniform cloak over his civvies and turning his collar back to front. He doesn't realise that if you are a cop and work shifts you sometimes need sleep and physical refreshment more than spiritual refreshment. I don't like civilian ministers. At least the police padre only calls us to church once a year and then we all have to go, from the top brass down to the lowest ranks, with me and my mates at the end of the procession. Civvies bore me! They are always shouting about their rights, but only between 10 am on Mondays and 4 pm on Fridays. The rest of the time they play golf or talk about it. I don't like the way everyone treats civilians as if they were human beings, just because they don't wear a uniform. Have you ever noticed that the civilian staff don't need a welfare officer. The only people that need a welfare officer for support and protection are the police officers. Significant? There's no doubt about it the police service and its staff are divided up into first and second class citizens. Have you ever had your photograph taken by a civilian photographer? I don't mean with a numbered board round your neck. Just look at the difference. (I've heard that they all work for passport photograph agencies in their spare time). I reckon I wouldn't be able to get out of the country with the photograph on my warrant card, and that's saying something nowadays!

If you think that I'm being unreasonable, biased, bigoted, bloody-minded or bloody stupid, let me ask you one final question, have you ever tasted civvy-made tea à la canteen? The last disgusted cop who was asked "Tea or coffee?" and said, "What's the difference?" was told "Two Pee". Which sums it up rather neatly, don't you think? No! they may be blonde, brunette, shapely, statuesque, or sport ringlets down to their shoulders, and that's just the men, I still don't care very much for civilians.

I wish I didn't have to join their ranks next September, after all I've only served for 40 years and 60 isn't really too old for a chief inspector, is it?.

                                                                Joe Kerr.

*   *   *

Knowing her husband's habit of sampling everything she baked, the wife left a note on a dozen cakes reading 'counted – one dozen'. When she returned two had disappeared and the note had been altered to read 'think metric'.

*   *   *

The mounted police everywhere are popular and in Glasgow this is particularly true; they are a part of city life. However, like people, horses can become set in their ways.

Recently, a mounted cop in the city centre saw a youth run from a shop in Gordon Street. The running youth paid no attention to the cop's command to stop and a chase ensued down Mitchell Street. It was like 'McCloud' of TV fame in Glasgow!

The suspect turned into Mitchell Lane with the horse cantering after him. However, the horse reached a certain point in the lane at which it stopped and no amount of urging by the rider could get it to start again.

There are no prizes for guessing that it had stopped at a back door from which it received its daily tit-bit!

E Sinclair

*   *   *

Bed & Breakfast on the House
The Thirstane Day Nursery in Great Western Road had a problem. They looked after children by day and harboured an unwelcome visitor at nights and at weekends. The staff liked the children, or most of them anyway, but they got a bit fed up with the night visitor who broke into the nursery four times during February and March. Not only did he break in but he usually cooked himself a meal and topped it off with a glass of Martini – if it was available.

The Crime Prevention Officer for the area decided to combat the problem with the aid of technology. He installed a burglar alarm, tested it and found it to be OK. He then left hoping that the intruder would break in over the weekend. He did. The alarm didn't work and the CPO was heartbroken to find that the crook had not only spent the weekend in the nursery but he had devoured $2\frac{1}{2}$ dozen eggs, bacon and anything else he could get his hands on. The faulty alarm was removed and the divisional commander detailed two plain clothes men to sit in the nursery overnight until the 'breaker was caught'.

On the second night of the watch their dominoe game was interrupted by a smashing of glass as the intruder made his entry. He was arrested, of course, and admitted all the previous 'breakings' at the nursery as well as others in the area. Not only was the Crime Prevention Officer delighted but his staff at the nursery was pretty happy too. They put their thoughts into rhyme and sent it to the divisional commander.
The poem read:
'To all the men of Marine Division
Our grateful thanks on your successful mission.

Kojak and Cannon couldn't have done better,
McCloud and possibly Pepper,
Alas, poor Tom with his wee black box,
He tried with all his might,
But not a 'bleep' or squeak was heard
All through the whole damn night
But nothing daunted he arranged
Two babysitters to guard our weans.
Two stealthy lads – honest and true,
They grabbed their man before he flew.
Sorry, boys, you couldn't maim him.
If we catch him next we'll castrate him.
To Hungry Horace, our Cad of the Month
Please pick a Judge that'll give him the crunch.
To one and all we extend our thanks
For a job well done through all the ranks.'

Not to be outdone the boys in the 'B' Division composed
a verse and these were the lines they sent back.

Dear Staff.
Thank you for your cheerful letter
It really made us all feel better
Your little rhyme has made us smile
Your effort really was worthwhile.

The ned was caught, we are delighted
His hopes of loot and grub we've blighted
Like you we hope his whack he'll cop
And a sharp edged Judge gives him the 'chop'.

Castration though is far too lenient
(he 'gaily' may find it quite convenient)
As men with kids, some time we've spent
Devising suitable punishment.

The fruits of our deliberation
Make nonsense of a mere castration
We'd fix him to a wall with chains
Confined with twenty screaming weans.

Some months of this, we guarantee
and he'd never come near a nursery
The punishment should fit the crime
And this we feel, would 'blow his mind'.

As to Kojak and the rest
Those boys have never stood the test
Your local cops are quite successful
Without a break for the commercial.

T Jamieson

*   *   *

For the following contributions I am indebted to Detective
Inspector Heaney of the Lancashire Constabulary. He has kindly
passed to me material he has been collecting. Credit is due to
members of the Lancashire Constabulary, the Police Review
and the magazine of the Police Federation, 'Police'.

Glaring over his glasses at the mousey little man in front of him
the magistrate sniffed: "You're a locksmith, are you? What
were you doing in that gambling den when the police raided it?"
The little man looked down sheepishly and said: "Your
honour, I was making a bolt for the door!"

*   *   *

Man telephones police station: "I would like to report some
extension ladders missing."
Reply: "We will takes steps to recover them!"

*   *   *

A young policewoman rang Southern Ireland whilst making
enquiries regarding a young girl missing from home. The
message was duly transmitted at the end of which the Irish
policeman asked the policewoman to give her name etc to
complete the record, which she duly did. The policewoman,
with true Lancashire Constabulary efficiency, also requested
the Irish policeman for his collar number and, after a short
pause, during which time one could almost hear his mind
ticking over, back came the answer – 15½!

*   *   *

Magistrate: "Is this the first time you've been up before me?"
Prisoner: "I don't know, your worship, what time do you
usually get up?"

Elderly lady to PC in Enquiry Office: "I've lost my cat."
PC: "Have you put an advertisement in the paper?"
Elderly lady: "Don't be daft, lad, he can't read!"

*   *   *

From time to time typographical errors are to be seen in the
best of publications. Not always are they corrected, and when
they are the correction occasionally makes things no better.
The following was recently noted in a professional publication.
"Suggestions for stuffing the Inspectorate will be passed on
immediately." In an ensuing edition there appeared a short
apologetic paragraph which went on to inform the readers that
it should have read: "Suggestions for staffing the Inspectorate
will be p.ssed on immediately."

*   *   *

The following conversation took place recently between a
caller and a constable at the police station:
Caller: "Is PC Smith in?"
Constable: "No, he's out on patrol."
Caller: "Will you leave him a message?"
Constable: "Yes, go ahead."
Caller: "Harry's dead. Can't meet you tonight. Friday will do."
Constable: "Is he expecting this news?"
Caller: "No, I don't think so."
Constable: "Who shall I say the message is from?"
Caller: "Me, Harry Stead."

*   *   *

**Who's a naughty boy then? (A light-hearted survey of the Traffic
Police and their prey?)**
Foreigners with a few exceptions such as detected and
apprehended drug traffickers, white slavers, international jewel
thieves and rapists, leave our pollution-drenched shores
sincerely under the impression that our police are wonderful.
So we are.
    They suffer the slings and arrows of outrageous motorists
and are frequently asked 'Instead of persecuting innocent

motorists why don't you go out and catch some burglars or train robbers or something?! The facts are that the motorist is hardly ever innocent, otherwise he or she wouldn't have been stopped in the first place, burglars are pretty thin on the ground and train robbers only emerge every third decade and someone else is chasing them anyway – that's why.

Little wonder then that some of the police who have the misfortune to come into contact with the motoring public are tempted to waive the terribly formal regulation greeting, chat and warning and substitute something less formal, like, for instance, 'What's up, Doc,' or 'Who's a naughty boy then?'

We have done a survey among both the police and the motorists. It would appear that as experience of dealing with delinquent motorists clocks up on an officer's tachometer, formality flies out of the exhaust, so to speak.

Most officers, probably because they are creatively frustrated by the disciplines of their job, like to inject a little originality into their work by developing their own techniques. There is one, for example, of religious leanings who, after warning a speeding motorist, will send him on his way with a blessing which involves making the sign of the cross. Another carries the business cards of a local undertaker which he gravely hands to bad drivers.

There is one traffic cop who once had a yearning to be an insurance salesman. He offers to sell offenders a sudden death policy – usual premium £10 for £10,000 cover, 'but for you, sir, £50 for £500 cover – because you are a bad risk.'

There is a Yorkshire constable who likes to be deliberately obtuse. He addresses all offending male motorists as 'Madam' or 'Miss'. Then excuses himself by saying: "Well you were driving like a bloody woman." He asks female drivers, regardless of age: "Does daddy know you've borrowed his car?" And there is the charmer who says: "Just think what would happen to that pretty face if you had an accident." He says that to the fellows too!

*   *   *

Dogberry in 'Police'

My Wicked Ex-Copper of the Month award has aroused some interest among editors and perhaps they will be a little more careful before handling some miscreant's brief and long forgotten association with the service. But what can I say about the *Evening Argus,* published in Brighton?

EX-POLICEMAN'S SON STOLE is the headline. It goes on: 'The son of a former police superintendent was fined £30 at Uckfield for theft. Lorry driver, E.B.A. . . . . ., 61 years, of Worthing, admitted stealing a box of glasses and 12 tins of soup while delivering frozen food to a grocer's shed at Framfield. It was his first conviction.'

It's not easy for a policeman's child to live down his past, is it?

*   *   *

Speaking at a London Luncheon, Mr Patrick Kavanagh, Deputy Commissioner, Metropolitan Police, recounted some of the ruses used by motorists to deceive traffic wardens. A car "not quite up to embassy standards," said Mr Kavanagh, was seen parked in Regent Street bearing CD plates. The driver's explanation to the suspicious warden was: "I am a cake deliverer." A man who left a stethoscope and a copy of the *Lancet* prominently on display got away with it from 'understanding' wardens until he was seen one day loading his car with dress samples.

A Mini driver who went to a lot of trouble to avoid getting a ticket made a habit of taking a wheel off his car and putting it into his boot, leaving a note on the windscreen to say that he had gone to get a puncture fixed. He was detected by a warden who, suspecting that he had been fooled by a similar note before, watched unseen while the motorist returned and took the perfectly good wheel and tyre out of the boot.

And then there was the regular customer who, far from wanting to dodge, asked to be sent a monthly account.

*   *   *

There are several Police Training Centres throughout the country and the following is an amalgam of student howlers. Though the list is not exhaustive it reflects a fair cross-section without being too technical.

1. An inquest is held on a DISEASED person to acertain cause of death.
2. Matters to be ascertained at an inquest: (a) how deceased died (b) WHO deceased died.

3. Identification can be by PHLORENSIC science.

4. Identification can be by remains – if dead.

5. Inquests – to ascertain . . . if, in the case of murder, he was dead before or at time of death.

6. Non-indictable offence is one that is not an indictable offence.

7. Dying declaration – the person making it must be dead.

8. Magistrates' function – to send summary cases to a HIRE court.

9. Manslaughter – example – husband comes home to find his wife in bed with another man, does his nut and kills the other man.

10. Injured horse – in any case, the PC should obtain the signature of the vet certifying death before the animal is killed.

11. A Common Lodging House is a place where destitute and homeless persons sleep together in one room.

12. Type of warrant – EXTRICATION warrant.

13. Reputed thief – one who is reputed of THIEVING.

14. Warning you would expect to find on crashed RAF plane fitted with ejector seat: "Red triangle with word "INJECTOR" printed inside.

15. Truncheon – should not be used unless the Constable thinks his life is likely to be extinct.

16. In a Juvenile Court there must be at least three Magistrates sitting together, male and female combined.

17. Leading question – a suggestive question.

18. Question: 'Name and explain the two types of hackney carriage.'
    Answer: 'One being powered by a motor of some sort and having electric lights and is totally enclosed, entrance or exit only by a door on either side, the other being drawn by other than mechanical power (eg horse drawn) not having electric obligatory lamps but usually having oil wick lamps. The vehicle usually has no roof whereby it is made to collapse to become very open.'

19. It is an offence to be drunk in charge of a child in a public place or highway whether by payment or otherwise.

20. The Coroner's Jury usually consists of 9 or 11 people (may be more than 11 but not less than 9).

21. What is a Common Police Service? Helping an old lady across the road.

22. All persons standing in the Identification parade must not be accused.

23. See if the killed person is dead.

24. Other Road Traffic Offence – being under the age of 17 without a licence.

25. Use of truncheon – aim for MUSSEL areas.

26. Points to remember when taking witness statement – take a negative statement if he knows nothing.

27. Identification Parades should not be held on Sundays, Christmas Days, Good Friday, Boxing Days, Easter Monday or Bank Holidays.

28. A hybrid offence is one for which you can be charged twice.

29. In the case of a dying declaration the person must be dead by the time of the court, and in the case of a deposition he need only be married before appearing.

30. If the owner cannot be contacted, a veterinary surgeon must be called. If he says it is too fatally injured to be moved, he can destroy it.

31. At a magistrates' court a student who had just left the Training Centre commenced his evidence as follows: "PC ? stationed at Blanktown!"

32. A student dealt with an offence of allowing cattle to stray on the highway and submitted a report to this effect which commenced as follows: "At 1.45 pm on Monday, 7th June, I was on duty in High Street, where I saw a brown cow straying on the highway. I approached the animal and said: "It is an offence to stray on the highway." I cautioned him and he replied "Bullocks."

33. When completing his evidence a student said: "That is my worship your evidence."

34. An Irish student was asked: "What is a pantechnicon?" He replied: "I'm not sure, but is it a coloured pancake?"

35. A new recruit in his first week at the training centre whilst carrying a bucket full of clothes brushes in his right hand was confronted by an advancing inspector. In a state of panic he saluted and emptied the brushes over himself.

36. A student instructor gave a lesson at a centre and after he had left the class the instructor asked his students how the lesson had progressed. Everyone, except one, agreed that it

had been a very good lesson. When asked why this particular student had not enjoyed the lesson he replied: "But I only respond to you, sergeant!"

37. One disgruntled student nailed a kipper under the commandant's chair.

38. One of the most difficult subjects for students at Police Training Centres to absorb is the legislation covering firearms, particularly so for the ladies.

   An instructor, recently, gave this lesson, and, towards the end, began to sense that some of his female students were still mystified. In an effort to establish just what had been learned, he decided to ask some general recap. questions. He picked upon one young female, and, thinking that he had better make it very simple for a start said: "Very well, let's go back over it generally to begin with. Can you tell me for instance, a difference between SHOTGUNS and AIR PISTOLS?" Looking rather hesitant, the female student replied: "Sergeant, the difference between a shotgun and an air pistol is that with an air pistol you can hold it in one hand, with a shotgun you need two!"

39. An alien cannot land unless he has a nationality and is not a citizen of the world.

40. Personation: Representing a person you are not in fact to be.

41. Reason for refusing the grant of a firearms certificate: Blind or having no arms.

42. Common law powers of entry: In immediate pursuit of the Commissioner of a serious crime.

43. Hearsay evidence is the evidence which is passed from mouth to mouth.

44. 'Knacker': Any person whose trade it is to kill cattle, but whose flesh is not for human consumption.

45. Practical involving constable telling father that his son had been killed in a road accident but there was some doubt as to the identity of the victim.
   Constable: "I have some bad news, your son is lying in the morgue, however, look on the bright side – it may not be him!"

46. Road Traffic Act – reason for suspecting alcohol in body:
    (a) he was driving erotically
    (b) he was driving irately
    (c) he was driving exotically.
47. PC: "I am arresting you for being drunk and disorderly."
    Offender: "But I'm not disorderly."
    PC: "No, but you will be when I arrest you."
48. Cruelty to animals – Can you be cruel to a tortoise?
    PC: "Not unless you give it shell shock!"
49. Report concerning woman stuck in lift:
    "We managed to exterminate her through the escape
    hatch."

*   *   *

The use of the English language or, perhaps the misuse of the
English language, is highlighted by a contribution from Edward
M Davis, Chief of Police, Los Angeles Police Department. He
refers to an article in the magazine of that department.

In this article comment is made on the standard of English.
It states: "Police recruits the world over, occassionally suffer
from a malady known in academic circles as 'spellingus and
grammartis incorrectus." Examples are given of what are
described as 'Pearls of Wisdom.' Some of the spelling errors
found indicate the presence of a phonetic alphabet, one
entirely unknown and, until now, unsuspected by the world
outside the Academy walls. A dictionary in this new recruitese
would include the following entries:

> Abbistoley – habitually
> Butlocks – rear portion of the anatomy
> Cafitiereir – a place to eat
> Camraws – used to take pictures
> Contence – something contained
> Crub – the edge of the sidewalk (pavement)
> Debut – something owed
> Exaim – to look at something closely
> Felmae – as mosed to lmae
> Fowl Night – as opposed to a nice day
> Huntch – a feeling about something
> Illeagle – unlawful; not a sick bird
> Jim Clothes – such as sweaty socks and tennis shoes

Loode – goes along with lascivious

Mikeraphone – scientifis instrument you speak into

Pance – Jim clothes that cover the butlocks on a fowl night

Pasted – as in "he pasted the exaim-ation"

Peril Harbor – a dock in danger

Preqant – exclusive condition of a felmae

Risk Lock – what to use on a loode person after an illeagle act

Seaced – what the loode person has been if a risk lock is used

Tatue – skin flicks

Textinige – technique (really!)

Vech, Vhecle, Vehichle, Vehechile – four types of transportation.

*   *   *

For statistical purposes activity logs are kept by operational constables. Of necessity these have to be brief and, sometimes brevity leads to misinterpretation; a few examples below:

Interview missing person.

Emergency call – complaint on numerous subjects and lost cat report.

Assisting at attempted suicide.

"Pig Licence" – written description below "recruiting enquiry."

Receive stolen property.

14 straying cattle of various genders.

Drunk lying flat out in telephone kiosk.

Fill car up with petrol.

Obscene phone call with policewoman.

Found lost bus and driver A57 Snake.

Transport re offender in case of damage (another P.c.).

Follow-up re cause of death by phone.

Attempt suicide at Heanor.

Observation for 'peeping tom'.

RTA Bent Lane – motor-cyclist hit cow – unconscious.

Attempt execution – Sudbury.

Still Britain's most famous policeman: Jack Warner as Dixon of Dock Green

The best-known of all actor-policemen is still surely Jack Warner, Sgt. 'Dixon of Dock Green' – a legend in his own right. No one policeman was respected and admired as much as this fine actor. During his long career he did much to give a good image of the ordinary policeman. Therefore it is a pleasure to record Jack's own version of his association with the police.

"My first real meeting with the police was long before the film 'The Blue Lamp' or the Television show 'Dixon of Dock Green'. It happened many years ago when I was a small boy cycling to school when I skidded under a big hay cart. It was being pulled by a very big cart horse which began lashing out with its very large hooves, and things looked very nasty for little Jack Waters – my legal name. The more I struggled the more the horse kicked out and if it had not been for the presence of mind of a policeman standing on the local police station steps, at Bow in the East End of London, who nipped smartly down and dragged me out of the way of that angry horse, I am quite sure I would not be writing this story for you now.

All my life since then has seemed to be mixed up with policemen and bicycles. I expect many remember my radio show at the beginning of the war in which I was a Cockney soldier. It was called 'Garrison Theatre' and one of my famous catch phrases was 'Mind my Bike'. So there you have the bike and the policeman and although Dixon is now finished, I will always remember with great affection that copper who saved my life at Bow.

When Sir Michael Balcon of Ealing Studios asked me if I would like to be a policeman in a film called 'The Blue Lamp' I jumped at the chance at once. I realised when I read the script that I would be shot in the first half-hour of the film and would disappear, but I still had a very strong feeling about the part, and this in spite of the fact that a lot of well-meaning friends said the part was too small and I should have a bigger one. I still insisted and the rest is now film history.

I saw the film in France, Germany and Greece, and I even saw it in Hong Kong on the way back from Korea in 1951, and, in each case the spirit of the shot policeman went right through to the end of the film. When I saw it in Greece, with my wife, I was sitting behind an old lady who started to cry when I was shot. She was making such a noise that the manager came over and whispered something in her ear, and when she turned round and saw me, she started to cry all the more. When I asked the manager what he had said he replied: "Well, I just said that you weren't dead, you were sitting right behind her." Poor old soul.

When we were making the film I was walking along one day, supposedly 'on the beat'. While walking towards the camera a car pulled up beside me and a man came over and said: "Excuse me, officer, can I leave my car here while I have a bit of lunch?" No sound was being recorded, so I said: "You can leave it there all day, it's nothing to do with me." The shot wasn't spoiled but I had to telephone the station at Paddington Green to tell them not to report him if a real copper came along.

With regard to the 'Dixon of Dock Green' show I have always been very grateful for the help and encouragement we always had from the Metropolitan Police as well as the City Police and those all over the country. But one of the most interesting aspects was the effect the programme had on children. I remember one time when I used to talk a lot about Road Safety at the end of the show. One evening I didn't mention it and I had a letter from a little girl saying: "Please will you say next week what you said last week about Road Safety because my brother didn't hear it and he takes more notice of you than he does of his father."

I once had a letter from an old lag who seemed to have spent most of his life in prison. He wrote: "Dear Sir, every time I see you in that uniform on television I think you are the very personification of justice: and I think that like justice, not only should you be done but you should be seen to be done." He probably meant it.

One of the nicest things that has ever happened to me was quite recently when I was invited to a police luncheon at the new Paddington Green Police Station in Harrow Road, London. There were many high-ranking officers there from Sir Robert Mark downwards and, when the lunch was finished, I was presented with a marvellous coloured print of the old police station at Paddington where we made 'The Blue Lamp'. Coming as it did from the Commissioner himself to the Station Sergeant at Dock Green I was very moved and that print will be one of my most treasured possessions."

*   *   *

Representative Howard W Smith of Virginia likes to tell the story of the County Prosecutor who wondered why a certain juror always voted for conviction. "Why do you vote that way?" the prosecutor asked the juror, "Is it the judge's charge, the brilliant summing-up by the prosecutor or what?" "No, I don't pay no attention to that stuff" said the juror, "I just look at them fellows in the case and say to myself, if they ain't guilty, what are they doing there?"

*   *   *

A lawyer was cross examining a witness, he asked: "And you say you called on Mrs Jones on May 2nd, now will you tell the jury just what she said?" "I object to the question," interrupted the lawyer on the other side. There was nearly an hour's argument between counsel and finally the judge allowed the question. "As I was saying," the first lawyer began again, "On May 2nd you called on Mrs Jones, now what did she say?" "Nothing," replied the witness, she was not at home".

*   *   *

When you have no basis for argument, abuse the plaintive. (Cicero 106 43 BC)

*   *   *

We are not won by arguments that we can analyse but by tone and temper by the manner which is the man himself. (Samuel Butler 1835–1902)

*   *   *

Bluster, Splutter, Question, Trammel, but be sure your argument is intricate enough to confound the Court. (William Wycherley 1640–1716)

*   *   *

A lawyer has no business with the justice or injustice of the cause which he undertakes unless his client asks his opinion and then he is bound to give it honestly. The justice or injustice of of the cause is to be decided by the judge. (Dr Samuel Johnson 1709–1784)

His defending solicitor knew that he was lying but was concerned only to extract the untruths in their correct order. (Sir William Connor (Casandra) 1909–1967)

*   *   *

Justice is what we get when the decision is in our favour. (Anon)

*   *   *

Justice is my being allowed to do whatever I like. Injustice is whatever prevents my doing so. (Samuel Butler 1835–1902)

*   *   *

I was never ruined but twice: once when I lost a law suit and once when I won one. (Voltaire 1694–1778)

*   *   *

Jansen got into trouble with the police and went to a lawyer. "If I win this case I will give you a thousand krona" he said. "Very well," said the lawyer, "Get some witnesses." Jansen got his witnesses and won his case. "Well," said the lawyer, "You won your case, what about my 1,000 krona?" "That's all right," said Jansen, "Get some witnesses."

*   *   *

"If the law supposes that," said Mr Bumble . . . "the law is an ass – an idiot." (Oliver Twist – Chapter 51)

*   *   *

The International Police Association was formed many years ago to promote friendship and a common understanding among police officers of many nations. Today it is a strong organisation and has as its official publication 'Police World!' The following are extracts from this magazine.

Constabulary Office,
Cheltenham
18 March 1841

Circular Order

The Serjeants and Constables are directed to wear their Old Uniforms on night Duty and wet days under their great Coats

and as there is but one pair of Trousers allowed to each man
for the present Year every attention must be paid to spare them
as much as possible and as the Character of the Force depends
much on the cleanliness and respectable appearance of the men
it will easily be perceived by frequent inspection of the Clothing
in what Sub District the best discipline and Order is maintained.

Signed: Anthony Thomas Lefroy
Chief Constable

*   *   *

Constabulary Office,
Cheltenham,
23 August 1842
Circular Order

The Superintendents of the Gloucestershire Constabulary
are informed that should any of the men be seen with their
Hair and Whiskers in a long and disgusting state as worn by
several at present they will be most severely punished.

Signed: Anthony Thomas Lefroy
Chief Constable

*   *   *

It has been mooted over the years that 'chain' letters should be
the subject of legislation because some of the worst had put
people in fear – the following is different.

"This chain letter was started by a man like yourself in the hope
that it might bring some happiness and relief to tired, bored
working men. Unlike most chain letters this won't cost you a
penny. Simply send a copy of this letter to five of your friends
who are equally tired and bored. Then bundle up your wife and
send her to the man whose name appears at the top of the list,
and add your name to the bottom of the list. When your name
appears at the top of the list you will receive 16,748 women.
Some of them are bound to be an improvement over what you
have had.

Have faith – do not break the chain. One man did and got his
wife back. A friend of mine recently received 946 women; he was
buried yesterday. It took the undertaker 36 hours to get the
smile off his face."

From the 'Evening Standard'

"I have always been convinced that Charlie Chaplin derived some of his comic inspiration from the antics of Paris traffic cops. This week I had proof of it. Driving around the Place-de-Concorde I was held up by an unaccustomed traffic diversion. At this point a policeman who was directing the diversion was brushed slightly by a car which ground to an instant horrified halt.

The policeman turned on the car in fury and kicked it hard on the grille. The car was undamaged but for the next two or three minutes the traffic piled up while the policeman hopped around on one foot."

★   ★   ★

GLOSSARY OF BAFFLEGAB

Technical jargon is not peculiar to commerce and management – we have it in the Police Service. The following is a list of some examples of the new art of Bafflegab:

A PROGRAMME	Any assignment that can't be completed by one telephone call.
CHANNELS	The trail left by inter office memos.
CONSULTANT (OR EXPERT)	Any ordinary guy more than 50 miles from home.
STATUS QUO	The mess we're in.
LIAISON OFFICER	A person who talks well and listens better, but has no authority to make a definite statement.
TO ACTIVATE	To make carbons and add more names to the memo.
TO IMPLEMENT A PROGRAMME	Hire more people and expand the office.
UNDER CONSIDERATION	Never heard of it.
UNDER ACTIVE CONSIDERATION	We're looking in the files for it.
A CONFERENCE	A place where conversation is substituted for the dreariness of labour and the loneliness of thought.

TO NEGOTIATE	To seek a meeting of minds without a knocking together of heads.
RE-ORIENTATION	Getting used to working again.
RELIABLE SOURCE	The guy you just met.
INFORMED SOURCE	The guy who told the guy you just met.
UNIMPEACHABLE SOURCE	The guy who started the rumour originally.
A CLARIFICATION	To fill in the background with so many details that the foreground goes under.
MODIFICATION OF POLICY	A complete reversal which nobody admits.
TO SPELL OUT	To break big hunks of bafflegab down into little hunks of bafflegab.
WE ARE MAKING A SURVEY	We need more time to think of an answer.
NOTE AND INITIAL	Let's spread the responsibility for this.
LET'S GET TOGETHER ON THIS	I'm assuming you're as confused as I am.
GIVE US THE BENEFIT OF YOUR PRESENT THINKING	We'll listen to what you have to say as long as it doesn't interfere with what we've already decided to do.
FURTHER SUBSTANTIATING DATA NECESSARY	We've lost your stuff. Send it again.
CONFIDENTIAL MEMORANDUM	There wasn't time to mimeograph
WILL ADVISE YOU IN DUE COURSE	If we figure it out, we'll let you know.

*   *   *

The following is a contribution from Supt. Michael Hirst of the Leicestershire Constabulary, which appeared in the "Police" magazine in December, 1977.

Never in the field of human conflict, or any other field, yard, garden or area for that matter, has so much been expected of so few by so many for so little as of the Police Service during 1977. Once again, we have found ourselves the meat in society's sandwich – which probably accounts for why I was bitten three times during the year. Politically we have kept the Fascist extreme right wing Nationalists from the throats of the International Racial Solidarists extreme left; economically we have separated the 'want to work' brigades from the 'want to picket' battalions; and socially prevented the multifariously deprived football hooligan from wreaking his vengeance on the rest of the capitalist non-caring society. On my Division you need a degree in politics to understand the duty sheet.

Professionally, our morale has been hit from two sides – on the one by the Civilian Complaints Board, and on the other by the Home Secretary. We have defended everyman's right to the freedoms of speech, picketing and withholding labour only to have our own requests to enjoy those same freedoms refused.

You see, I didn't join for all this aggravation – quite the contrary. Had I wanted excitement I could have stayed as the Hit Man with the WRVS. I envisaged police work as the occasional juvenile bicycle thief the odd shoplifter, snooker in the Divisional Club and a free front seat at the local football ground. Now, at the end of another year of policing what is supposed to be one of the most stable societies in Western Europe, I feel as if I've been in the charge of the Light Brigade and had to carry a wounded horse back. Heaven help us if our society ever becomes unstable.

The other lasting memory of 1977 is the divisional work to rule – yes, militancy raised its ugly head. It all began when the cook reduced the canteen breakfast sausage quota from two to one. As a famous philosopher once said: 'I don't like canteen sausages but I'll fight to the death for every officer's right to two if he wants them'. These were our sentiments entirely. Militant action – the word flashed through the station faster than the rumour that the Woman Superintendent had become a Go-Go dancer. We formed a Citizens' Committee to decide on our course of action. I was all for taking the new red haired woman Sergeant hostage (at my place) but I was out-voted.

Instead we decided to fight fire with fire. Canteen breakfasts include free bread and free tea – and that's where we hit them. The plan was to bankrupt the local authority (well, it seemed a good idea at the time). In three days we ate 870 loaves and drank 500 gallons of tea – and there were only 12 of us.

But the revolution had its casualties: two men almost drowned, a traffic pointsman wet his pants and PC Guevera who had been stuffing slices of bread up his tunic raised his body temperature so high that the bread hardened and we had to cut him free with a hacksaw.

At the same time as the canteen campaign we began a Divisional work to rule for Federated Ranks. This comprised setting absolute minimal standards of work and not exceeding them. Unfortunately it fell through as the Inspectors and Sergeants found themselves doing 50% more than they normally did. Nevertheless, the general air of mutiny persisted throughout the week. Everybody refused to play cards with the Chief Inspector, which rather backfired on us as we realised too late they were his cards and we all applied for Traffic Department much to the annoyance of Personnel and the delight of Chief Superintendent Traffic who normally has to offer men bribes to join him.

At the beginning of the second week it happened – the Divisional Commander returned from leave. He has a paternalistic approach to leadership and anyone who has seen "The Godfather" will know exactly what I mean. He brought it all to an end with just two words which in police circles separate the militants from the moderates, the proletariat from the intelligentsia, the ambiguous from the ambitious – Promotion Boards.

It was all over in a twinkling. The militants were put on foot beats and the qualified officers sentenced to six months each in the Community Relations Branch, which we all felt was a bit severe. So much for the revolution. If the Czars had thought of promotion boards Lenin would still be on a foot beat and getting just the one sausage with his breakfast.

But all in all 1977 has passed breathtakingly quickly. Is it a full twelve months since I was extolling Chief Constables to speak out for the Service? May I just say to those who have stood up to be counted this year – Well done, chappies! But next year, perhaps if you could, like, all get it together more? Just so that it appears that we all actually belong to the same Service instead of 43 independent and private security organisations. Otherwise those naughty faceless Home Office men will start pushing us around again.

Leslie Charteris, the creator of the famous 'The Saint', writes:
I have often been accused of taking too much mickey out
of the police in my stories – and especially out of Scotland Yard,
as personified by Chief Insp Teal, the Saint's long-time
adversary.

I always point out that the Saint, as a modern Robin Hood,
and the hero, has to come off best, to keep the readers happy,
and must therefore make rather a monkey out of Teal – just as
in the typical detective story, the brilliant amateur always
makes the police professional look stupid. But I plead that it's
all done in a spirit of good fun.

And yet, if it's any justification for some of the digs I have
taken at the fuzz, I do treasure one item which can be authenti-
cated from the official transcript, and which I was privileged
to hear with my own ears many years ago, when as a reporter
I was covering the trial of Mrs. Elvira Barney, which was quite a
'cause celebre' in its day. The lady was accused of fatally
shooting her boy friend. Her defence was, that in the course of
a quarrel, he had produced a gun and threatened to do
something desperate with it, that she had tried to take it away
from him, and that in the resulting struggle it went off and
killed him.

A police witness was in the box, and the examination went
exactly as follows:

Counsel: "Was this gun examined for fingerprints?"
Detective: "Yes, Sir."
Counsel: "Whose fingerprints did you find?"
Detective: "My own."
So help me!

The following is a good example of the Saint verses Claud
Eustace:

The story of the Old Bailey trial reached Palma about six
weeks later, in an ancient newspaper which Patricia Holm
produced one morning.

Simon Templar was not at all interested in the story; but he
was vastly interested in an illustration thereto which he
discovered at the top of the page. The press photographer had
done his worst; and Chief Insp Teal the hero of the case,
caught unawares in the very act of inserting some fresh chewing
gum in his mouth as he stepped out on to the pavement of

Newgate Street, was featured looking almost libellously like an infuriated codfish afflicted with some strange uvular growth.

Simon clipped out the portrait and pasted it neatly at the head of a large plain postcard. Underneath it he wrote:

Claud Eustace Teal, when overjoyed,
Wiggled his dexter adenoid;
For well-bred policemen think it rude
To show their tonsils in the nude.

"That ought to come like a ray of sunshine into Claud's dreary life," said the Saint, surveying his handiwork.

He may have been right; for the postcard was delivered in error to an Assistant Commissioner who was gifted with a particularly acid tongue, and it is certain that Teal did not hear the last of it for many days. – *Published by PAN BOOKS*

* * *

Surely the best known author connected with the humorous side of the legal profession is Henry Cecil. Unfortunately, he has passed away but his wife was pleased to give her permission to present the following extracts.

His book "Brothers in Law" and the many others in the series, with the Cecil humorous approach, must have been read by countless millions. No book on humour touching upon the law would be complete without examples from his work. Here is an extract from "Brothers in Law" which epitomise the hilarious, yet warm, style of his writing:

They discussed the other milestones in a career at the Bar; then they talked about County Courts.

"What's this judge like?" asked Roger.

"Well, fortunately," said Henry, "there aren't any others like him today. I don't mean by that that he's a bad judge. He isn't. But he's very inconsiderate. Furthermore, he's peppery, pompous and conceited, but he's quite a good judge for all that, though not as good as he thinks he is. Incidentally, one of the funniest things I ever heard happened in front of him. Like to hear?"

There were three main characters in the story which Henry told Roger. The first was a barrister called Galloway, a well-intentioned, very serious and literally-minded man. The second was a former County Court judge called Musgrave.

"He's dead now," said Henry. "He was a nice old boy and

quite a good judge when he tried a case, but he was a wicked old man and wouldn't sit after lunch."

"What d'you mean?" asked Roger.

"What I say. He wouldn't sit after lunch. He spent part of the morning either making people settle cases or adjourning them for one reason or another and finally he tried what was left and rose at lunch-time. Very rarely he came back after lunch, but usually he made some excuse for postponing any case which hadn't finished by lunch-time until another day. I liked him, but he certainly was naughty. Well, one day Galloway had a case in front of Musgrave. It was an accident case which would have been likely to occupy a considerable part of the day. The judge had a medical referee sitting beside him to advise. When I say sitting, well, it was arranged that he should sit. The only question in the case was whether a man's illness had been caused by the accident, but a good deal of evidence would have had to be given about it. Before the judge sat he sent for the doctors who were being called on each side and told them to have a word with the medical referee. After they'd had a chat for ten minutes or so, the judge went in to see them himself. Five minutes later he came into court, sat down and announced that there would be judgement in the case for the defendants with costs.

"But . . ." said the unfortunate Galloway, who was appearing for the plaintiff.

"But what?" said the judge, quite severely.

"But . . ." repeated Galloway.

"If that's all you have to say, Mr. Galloway, I'll have the next case called," and this was duly done.

"Well, of course, the plaintiff wasn't going to take that lying down. His case had never been tried. The judge had no doubt acted upon what the doctors had told him behind closed doors. It was a complete denial of justice. So the plaintiff appealed to the Court of Appeal and Galloway started to tell their Lordships all about it. He hadn't gone very far with the story before the president of the Court, Lord Justice Brand, said:

"It's very difficult to believe that this really happened. Naturally, I'm not doubting your word, Mr. Galloway, but how can it have happened as you say without your saying something to the judge?"

"I did say something, my Lord."

"Oh – what was that?"

" 'But', my Lord."

"Yes, Mr. Galloway?"

" 'But', my Lord."

"But what, Mr. Galloway?"

"Just 'but', my Lord."

"I'm afraid I'm out of my depth," said another Lord Justice. "Are you still addressing us, Mr. Galloway?"

"Yes, my Lord."

"Then what did you mean when you said 'but' to my brother?"

"That was what I said, My Lord."

"I know you did, twice. But why?"

"I couldn't think of anything else to say, my Lord."

"Now, look," said Lord Justice Brand. "Let us get this straight. You didn't say 'but' to us . . .?"

"Oh, yes, he did," said Lord Justice Rowe.

"I know, I know," said Lord Justice Brand. "Please let me finish. The 'but' you said to us was the 'but' you said to the learned County Court judge, or to put it more accurately, it was another 'but' but the same word. 'But' is what you said to the County Court judge."

"Yes, my Lord," said Galloway.

Lord Justice Brand sat back in his chair triumphantly.

"But," said Lord Justice Rowe, "if I may be forgiven the use of the word, but is that all you said to the learned judge?"

"Yes, my Lord, just 'but'."

"But it doesn't mean anything."

"I didn't get a chance to say anything more, my Lord, and I was too flabbergasted."

"Really, Mr. Galloway," said Lord Justice Brand. "When I was at the Bar, I considered it to be my duty in the interests of my client to stand up to the judge and, if necessary, to be rude to him, yes, to be rude to him. I cannot believe that counsel of your experience would allow a thing like that to happen unchallenged."

"In the end, of course, they allowed the appeal and sent the case back to the County Court to be properly heard before another judge, but not before poor Galloway's mildness had been further criticised.

"A week later he had an accident case before Boyle – the judge you're going to meet. Galloway was appearing for the plaintiff. He got up and started to open the case to the jury, explaining to them where the accident happened and so on. He was just saying:

"Now, members of the jury, at what juncture the defendant's car without any warning of any kind whatsoever . . ." when the judge interrupted:

"Mr. Galloway, might I have a plan, please?"

"Be quiet," said Galloway and continued to address the jury. "And without any warning of any kind whatsoever . . ."

'Just as the Court of Appeal could not believe what was said to have happened in Musgrave's Court, Boyle couldn't believe he'd heard Galloway right. Galloway was a polite man and his behaviour was normally impeccable.

"I really can't follow this without a plan," said Boyle.

"Will you be quiet," said Galloway and started to go on addressing the jury. But not for long. This time the judge had no doubt what had been said.

"Have you taken leave of your senses, Mr. Galloway?" he said angrily. "How dare you speak to me like that!"

"Well, your Honour," said Galloway. "I was told last week by the Court of Appeal that it was my duty to be rude to the judge." '

Henry Cecil, 1955

*   *   *

Richard Gordon is to the medical profession what Henry Cecil is to lawyers, judges and policemen. In this extract from "Doctor at Large" the hero has a brush with the law.
The journey north was exciting, for neither the car – which I had christened 'Haemorrhagic Hilda' – nor I had been on the road for some time. Hilda was originally an expensive limousine, but now she was constructed of so many spare parts that I thought of her fondly as the bastard of some noble line. Her vertical windscreen, which opened horizontally across the middle, was colourful with rainbows and bright with stars; there was worm in the dashboard, where all the dials pointed to zero except the engine temperature, which was stuck at boiling; her furnishings had been replaced by a former owner and now

consisted of a pair of bucket seats from an old baby Austin perched on a fruit-box in front, and an ordinary small domestic horsehair sofa in the back. Behind the sofa were pieces of sacking, some old gnawed bones, a yo-yo, and scraps of newspaper prophesying the fall of Ramsay MacDonald's government. The front windows would not open and the back windows would not shut. Birds had nested under the roof, and mice under the floorboards.

The mechanical part of Haemorrhagic Hilda aroused my clinician's interest rather than my alarm. The engine produced more rales, sibili, and rhonchi than a ward of asthmatics, and the steering gear, which had a wheel fit for a London bus, was afflicted with a severe type of locomotor ataxia. The only pleasant surprise was the horn. This was a long silver trumpet creeping from the windscreen to coil comfortably over the bonnet and front mudguard, which on squeezing the rubber bulb sounded like feeding-time in the seal pool. Hilda's other surprisingly good point was her brakes, which I shortly had a chance of demonstrating.

Outside Stony Stratford a police car waved me to the roadside.

"You the owner of this vehicle?" the policeman demanded, taking my licence.

"And proud of it," I said cheerfully.

"I suppose you know there are regulations concerning the roadworthiness of motor vehicles?" he said in the tone used by Customs officers asking you to open the other suitcase. "Is the vehicle equipped with an efficient braking system?"

"Brakes? Absolutely wonderful, officer. She can pull up on a postage stamp."

"I am going to test the truth of your statement. Proceed along the highway at a reasonable speed. I will follow, and when I blow my horn apply your brakes."

"Right-ho," I said bravely.

I swung the engine, wondering what was going to happen: if the police decided to hound Hilda off the road, I would not only arrive late but lose the greater part of my working capital as well.

After I had travelled a few hundred yards my thoughts were interrupted by the urgent blast of a horn behind me. As I drove the brake-pedal into the floorboards, I realised that it was not the policeman, but a Bentley sweeping past our procession at eighty. There was a crash behind and my windscreen fell on to the bonnet. As Haemorrhagic Hilda had been built in the same spirit as the Pyramids, she suffered only another dent in the rear mudguard; but the police car lay with its wheels turned out like flat feet, bleeding oil and water on to the roadway.

"You'll hear more about this," the policeman kept muttering, as I dressed the small cut on his nose. I gave him a lift to the next telephone box and continued my journey in an unreasonably cheerful frame of mind."

First published by Michael Joseph

*   *   *

A close affinity has grown up between crime reporters and the police; there is an understanding between them. Crime reporters in their 'privileged' position get to know policemen just as they are, they see their strengths; they see their weaknesses but, above all, they, like the police, can see the funny side of the 'job'. Some years ago Bernard Scarlett and Norman Lucas wrote a fine book on the history of the Flying Squad. One chapter dealt with the humorous side of the squad's life and I am pleased to give this extract:

Members of the public seeking light relief within the pages of their daily newspapers cannot expect to find it in a report of a crime – except, perhaps, in rare court reports. The retailing of any criminal event is usually tinged with gloom and seldom is it possible, for reasons of space, to publish the humorous story behind the story.

The overall impression given is one of the police and the criminals locked in a fierce war of attrition with no quarter given or mercy shown. In reality, the picture is sometimes far less bleak. The war is, of course, relentlessly pursued by both sides and hard knocks are given and received, especially between the Flying Squad men and their natural enemies, the really professional criminals. Even so, humour can creep into the strange relationship between the two forces.

It is in the battle of wits that one common denominator links both sides – intuition or sixth sense. Without this, a Flying Squad officer would be a lost detective, for the development of this strange sixth sense is reflected in his record as a thief catcher. In the case of the hunted criminal, the extra initiative of self-preservation fashions the chances of liberty or detection and his sixth sense represents something akin to a built-in early warning system.

South London Billy has a highly sensitive early warning system. On one occasion, he left his usual haunts to "case a joint" – the home of a wealthy Member of Parliament – in a quiet street in the centre of the division bell area around Smith Square, Westminster.

There was nothing particularly furtive about his appearance or his actions in the mid-afternoon of a hot summer's day as Billy strolled among the sightseers on Westminster Bridge. As he stood on the pavement at the entrance to Cannon Row – the narrow lane behind Parliament Street that leads to the main gates of the old Scotland Yard – he leisurely lighted a cigarette.

He glanced idly up at Big Ben and then moved along with the crowd to the corner of Parliament Square where, still with the crowd, he waited on the pavement edge for a uniformed policeman to halt the traffic so that pedestrians could cross the street.

It was Billy's act of lighting a cigarette that had brought about a silent clash between two rival early warning systems. By pure coincidence, as he applied the match, the then head of the Flying Squad at that time, walked out of the Yard and even over a distance of 150 yards, he was able to recognise the crook. "That's Billy," he mused, "Now what's he doing on this side of the river?"

Without altering his pace, he took to the route Billy had followed earlier – along Derby Gate, into Parliament Street and towards Parliament Square.

He reached the corner of the square in time to see his quarry strolling past the statue of Oliver Cromwell outside Westminster Hall. Keeping almost 200 yards behind, the Yard man continued to shadow Billy past the House of Lords and down to Millbank.

More than once, Billy turned round. He reached the end of Lambeth Bridge and appeared to be undecided. Then he shrugged his shoulders and began to cross the bridge. He reached the centre span and stopped. He leaned on the parapet and gazed at the Thames.

He looked back to Millbank on the north side. He could see

no-one "suspicious". But Billy's sixth sense was working overtime. He abandoned his operation and hurried back to the South Side, where his presence in the streets was part of the day to day scene.

A few days later, the head of the Squad called at a public house in South London and found himself facing Billy in the bar. "Have a drink, guv'nor?", the crook's invitation was accompanied by a cheerful friendly grin.

"Thanks, I will," his smile was disarming, "and what have you been up to lately?"

"Nothing, as you know very well," grumbled Billy. "How can I work with your lot watching me all the time?" In strange, vague terms, he went on to describe his abortive expedition to Westminster. "I never see nobody, guv, but I could tell I was being tailed, so I beat it back here."

The Squad Chief's expression was enigmatic. "You're growing old and imagining things," he said.

Some weeks later, the two met again, quite casually. On that occasion, the boot was on the other foot and it was his turn to feel discomfited.

The Squad had received a tip along the underworld grapevine that the home of a wealthy Covent Garden merchant was going to be raided while the merchant was attending an important Masonic function.

A Flying Squad team was briefed and sent to the house which stood in acres of rolling countryside in Berkshire. They worked out details of their stake-out and, having several hours to wait before the scheduled time of the raid, decided to relax.

The merchant, grateful to the officers who were going to guard his home during the night, provided deck chairs and drinks on the lawn. When the hour approached for the merchant to leave for London, the deck chairs were stacked away and in the dusk, the Squad detectives took up their positions behind bushes and in the shadow of outbuildings.

They were prepared for a long wait plus eventual action. But the vigil was to last until the early hours of the morning when the merchant returned home and without incident. Wearily, they returned to their cars and to London, grumbling about the unreliability of the "Snout".

As Billy sipped a cool pint of beer, there was a twinkle in his eye when innocently, he asked: "Been having a busy time, then?"

"No, it's been very dull," was the reply.

"Oh – Mm, I heard you'd been trying your luck in Berkshire," said Billy, innocently studying the froth of his glass.

"Berkshire?" echoed the Yard Chief, "what about Berkshire?"

"Aw, come off it, Guv'," rejoiced the little crook. "Me and the boys went for a picnic after the races at Windsor and we seen your lads living it up. Sunbathing on a lawn and all that. Through the bins it was easy to recognise their faces from two fields away. We was wondering what you was doing so we drove back to the Smoke. You lot 'ave all the luck . . ." He wandered off chortling, leaving behind a very embarrassed detective.

HUMOUR AND THE POLICE REVIEW

All professions have their own periodical, magazine or newspaper; the Police Service is no exception. Published weekly is the Police Review which chronicles events, up-dates readers on professional matters and provides a forum of interchange of views between members of the service country-wide. It is a serious, responsible paper but does not exclude humour, indeed scattered through its pages may be found cartoons, essays and articles with a humorous base directed, of course, at the service.

Staff Appraisal has been a part of management for many years.
It is an indefinite science but a necessary part of Police selection procedures.
Below is a 'send-up' of this system.

Performance Factor	Far Exceeds Jobs Requirement	Exceeds Job Requirements	Meets Job Requirements	Needs Some Improvement	Does Not Meet Requirements
Quality	Leaps tall buildings with single bound	Must take running start to leap over tall buildings	Can only leap over buildings with no spires	Crashes into buildings when attempting to jump	Cannot recognise tall buildings
Timeliness	Is faster than a speeding bullet	Is as fast as a speeding bullet	Is not as fast as a bullet	Would you believe a slow bullet?	Wounds self with bullet
Initiative	Is stronger than a locomotive	Is stronger than a bull elephant	Is stronger than a bull	Shoots the bull	Smells like a bull
Adaptability	Walks on water constantly	Walks on water in emergencies	Washes with water	Drinks water	Passes water in emergencies
Communication	Talks with God	Talks with Angels	Talks to himself	Argues with himself	Loses those arguments

WOLL?

THERE are unseen problems inherent in the use of cycles. Consider this: two officers, Curly Wee and Gussey Goose (I'm sorry, they were named after two cartoon characters who appeared in the Liverpool Echo about 25 years ago), set out on cycles to their respective patrols. On the way they come across Desperate Dan, the Milkbar Man, smashing up the local milkbar in the course of a dispute over the ingredients of a Knickerbocker Glory. They arrest Desperate Dan, and being officers of some independence and initiative, secure him by hand-cuffing him between the two cycles, and return to the station with Desperate Dan trotting in the middle. They reach the corner of the High Street and Market Street. Curly Wee turns right, Gussy Goose, left. Desperate Dan is put to some inconvenience and subsequently complains. Now then, assuming that both the left turn and the right turn would have brought the trio to the station in the same amount of time, against whom is the complaint registered?

Don't let this put you off riding cycles.

On being asked to play for
the station rugby team

YOU will be seated one day in the Canteen. You have finished your Poulet a la Creme and are sipping your Chablis before making that difficult choice between Beignets Souffles or baked jam roll with custard; you will be approached by a Welshman. He will have a broken nose, and part of one ear missing. He will speak in a soft lilting voice. "Bach", he will say, "What about a fine lad like you playing for the station this Thursday in a friendly rugby match. Don't have to know much, most of us are beginners. Bit of fun, see?" The Welshman has chosen his time carefully, he may even have arranged with the wine waiter to spike your Chablis. (Yes, some Welshmen will stoop even that low). You will be feeling relaxed, cordial. You have a vision of yourself running smoothly along the green turf in a striped shirt and white shorts. You score the winning try, you are a natural born wing; next month, the Force team, perhaps later, New Zealand, the standing ovation at Cardiff Arms Park. That's the vision. The reality of the sport in which you have been invited to participate is a crude battle on a quagmire in horizontal sleet, between thirteen men in track suits whose captain and team manager are at the wrong ground with all the shirts and shorts, and seventeen men in assorted colours who have taken advantage of a short sighted referee. If you fall over, you will be trodden on by both sides indiscriminately, although your own side will try to avoid damage to your hands so that you will be able to purchase drink at a later stage.

Do not try to argue with a Welshman. You need a single unanswerable objection; thus. "Actually, my people are Surrey people, and we rather like hockey". The Welshman will not speak to you again. He may spit in your Chablis, but you have saved yourself from Hell.

Choosing the wrong wine with the sausage and mash

It may well be that the young officer coming in wet from his traffic point and entering a canteen where the waiters do not know him may succumb to the common temptation to order the '68 Bordeaux with his sausage (two pork) potato (mashed) and onion, 45p. His mistake will soon become apparent by the waiter's insolent sneer, and the sudden break in the conversation at the surrounding tables. At some stations he may be approached by the relief inspector with the suggestion that he dine in the stables to avoid giving further offence. The quick witted can turn such a situation to their advantage. "Sir, you wrong me greatly. A chap merely requires something red and palatable in which to dunk the occasional slice of onion. Waiter! The Riesling, and look sharp about it."

On how to pass the first two hours of early turn

THIS IS the best time of day for dealing with local vampires.
Too many young officers, called to a sudden death, and
noticing the tell-tale puncture marks in the victim's throat,
write out the standard vampire report, and issue the usual
crime prevention leaflet about keeping plenty of garlic about
the house. The good policeman can do more than this. Have
a good look round your local churchyards. You won't come
across a vampire in the marble slab and pious angel type of
cemetery; what you're looking for is a deserted burial place
that has wisps of fog drifting between broken gravestones
even in the height of summer. If there's an underground
vault, so much the better. Inspect the surfaces and edges of
each monument; that used by the vampire will be free from
weeds and moss (because they don't have a chance to grow if
the blessed thing is opened overnight, surely you can work
that out for yourself) then a quick flip of the lid, a sharp stake
through the heart, and another clear up for the crime book.
You must have a sharpened stake, trying to cut a point on
your truncheon with a penknife at the last minute can only
produce frustration and lengthy explanations at the next
parade at which you are required to produce it. May I also
caution you against applying for a Home Office Permit for
an exhumation? Whenever I've done this in the past, there
have been inexplicable delays, and when the permit
eventually arrives, THE VAMPIRE HAS BEEN MOVED.
I am not alleging that there is a vampire in the Home Office,
but records show that there is precious little overtime worked
there during the times of the full moon. Which brings me to
Wolfmen. I can't give you much help with this one; whenever
I've found a Wolfman on my ground, I've put in for a
transfer. If you get bitten by a Wolfman, you've had it, the
most you can hope for is a transfer to a protection point at
the Transylvanian Embassy.

SELECTION BOARDS

A DISCREET white sling about the left arm is a great help. make sure that the material used is clean and starched, a tatty sling is unpleasant for the board. No-one will ask you the nature of your injury, as no senior officer will ever admit to a colleague that he does not know everything that ought to be known about a candidate. You will gain the sympathy of the board before you start, and a reference during the interview to "my recent contretemps with the United supporters" will set their mind at ease and add to your credit. (By the way, always use one or two French words during an interview; members of a board like to be thought of as cultured.) This particular ploy can be overworked. At one board, five of the six candidates wore bandages, plasters, or slings, one even, unsportingly, came on crutches; the board had no option but to pick the sixth and only fit candidate.

A variation of this is "Hobson's Dash". The now legendary Hobson, in the course of an interview for a vacancy in the section that arranges pre-war accident records into date order rather than numerical order, was stuck for the answer to a certain question, and solved the problem by leaping through the nearby window with a yell of "They're stealing the chief constable's Begonias!" He got the job because of his obvious initiative and ability, having chased the imaginary thieves out of sight, and having carefully uprooted two begonias shortly before the interview.

On being called to a cat up a tree

DO NOT jump up and down, waving the Helmet, and calling "Here, Pussy, Pussy". This is not consistent with the dignity of the Force. Borrowing a nearby garden hose and attempting to flush it from its perch can have a number of undesirable consequences. A weak jet may result in your drenching the line of washing in the neighbouring garden; a too powerful jet may lead to the moggy being balanced at the end of the hose like a ping pong ball in a fairground shooting gallery. Never climb up the tree yourself. The cat invariably escapes, and you are then stuck up the tree. When the subsequent emergency call reaches the station "P.C. trapped in tree" the lads have a good laugh about the misprint and leave you there until booking off time.

The correct course when called to a treed moggy is the brisk approach, rapid assessment, and authoritative statement: 'That is not a cat, it is a bird in cat's clothing. Leave it alone and it will fly away". Stride confidently to the corner of the road, then run like hell.

On making your first arrest

WOLL?

DO NOT raise the truncheon high in both hands and bring it down amidships on the prisoner in the manner of a knight wishing to slice the head off a seasoned old dragon. A polite "Sir, you appear to be offending against the laws of this community. I fear that unless you offer some plausible explanation for your tyre lever being in the top of this church collection box, I shall have to escort you to the police station" will usually bring forth the rejoinder "You have caught me, bang to rights officer. Clap the cuffs upon these outstretched wrists, for I have done wrong". Should his response be less frank than this, be ready to raise the truncheon high etc.

Now bringing the prisoner to the station. Some officers, carried away by the excitement of the first knock, arrange for some ensemble such as the Black Dyke Mills Band to precede them back to the station. This smacks of ostentation. Nor will the station sergeant want to delay taking the charge until the television cameras are ready to record you giving evidence of arrest. Remember, it may be your first, but the station sergeant and prisoner have seen it all before.